The Pocket Book of Wild Food

By Paul Peacock

Published by The Good Life Press Ltd. 2008

ISBN 978 1 90487 126 2
A catalogue record for this book is available from the British Library.

Published by
The Good Life Press Ltd.
PO Box 536
Preston
PR2 9ZY

www.goodlifepress.co.uk
www.homefarmer.co.uk

Set by The Good Life Press Ltd.
Illustrations © by Paul Peacock
Printed and bound in Great Britain
by Cromwell Press

The Pocket Book of Wild Food

5 petals
all yellow

Primrose

Much
veined leaf
dark green
with some
yellow

By Paul Peacock

Dedication

For Trevor Sutton
whose British bird paintings continue to inspire

Contents

white flowers
as umbels.

Leaves in 3's

Ground Elder

Square or
angular stem

Many
Serrations

Preface

I make no apology for the simplicity of this book. I imagine the reader to be a person who has ventured frequently into the country or local park and wondered what of the landscape they see around them is edible. What is presented here is a very simple collection of plants, animals and fungi that can be had in any reasonable quantity without messing up either the countryside or their own health. It doesn't give descriptions of plants that can be easily confused with poisonous species, and this means there are some gaping omissions. Sweet cicely, for example, is a brilliant plant, but is so much like hemlock you wouldn't believe it – especially as you listen to the laughs of the doctor as he pumps your stomach and starts your blood transfusion.

So, more than anything, I want my reader to remain safe. Maybe in some other year I might bring out a complete modern herbal of edible wild plants. In the meantime there are plenty available in the libraries.

There is not much by the way of eating animals and road kill, just a passing mention really. You could, I suppose, wander through the countryside with a ferret stuffed down your trousers, just in case, but on the whole people who like to do that sort of thing are already prepared. Hopefully people will also find the odd references to sea fishing and shrimping useful too.

When you think of food from the wild, a number of things come to mind. Does he mean fish or plants or mushrooms? Surely he doesn't mean chasing wildebeest in some far distant African plain or to sit, crouched and shivering, over a hole in the retreating ice of deepest Canada?

I suppose that the number of places you can collect or kill food from the wild are few indeed, but it is the ability to recognise what is edible and what isn't that gives a sense of empowerment in an age where our food is so often packaged and controlled.

This book is not about survival. It is about reconnecting with food from the wild that tastes good. You can eat grass, but it tastes like grass! You can eat the bark of birch trees, but you wouldn't want to. But you can collect grass seeds and make a loaf of bread, and you can tap into a birch tree in the spring and ferment the juice, then fade away into a far distant land where sleep and happy thoughts mingle. In short, it makes great wine.

It is possible to eat well on the plants that grow in profusion around us. But you do need to be careful, knowledgeable (to a degree), skilful and bold. It has taken three generations of living away from the land to all but destroy our ability to enjoy wild plants as food. And let's be honest; the thought of eating a plate of fat hen or boiled nettles doesn't really appetize, does it? But, with a little self discipline regarding our appetite, the quantities we consume and what we perceive to be good food, then the benefits of wild food are amazing – particularly wild plants.

If you are going to take an evolutionary point of view, and it is not always welcome, then there is one thing about eating wild plants that is very useful, and that is their seasonality. If we have evolved for many hundreds of generations on certain plants being available at certain times of the year, then surely these plants will have played an important role in our nutritional requirements. Dandelions that grow in the spring are full of vitamins and plant proteins that are especially good for us, particularly when it comes to recharging our bodies after the long winter, and particularly for our renal and digestive systems. Fat hen is so filled with protein and minerals that it is much healthier to eat than cabbage.

But it is not only food that wild plants provide. Many a strong rope, a suit of clothes, bedding, paper or even a home has been made from nettles. The fibres in this plant are particularly useful in rope making. But then the nettle, as we have already heard, makes excellent food and is very nutritous and tasty to boot. On top of this, to quote the Plants for a Future database, "…the whole plant is antiasthmatic, antidandruff, astringent, depurative, diuretic, galactogogue, haemostatic, hypoglycaemic and a stimulating tonic."

To perhaps illustrate this in a more palatable way, the blackberry seems to be as good a plant as any. Everyone likes blackberries and they grow everywhere. You often find gardeners complaining that they have a patch of brambles they need to clear on their land and are seen as a complete pain. However, the truth is they form an impenetrable hedge against animal movements, provide excellent security for the urban garden and are not only delicious to eat but also have excellent healing qualities. You can make a restorative tea from the dried leaves and the young shoots, peeled, are wonderful in salads.

When I started thinking about this book I wondered if it might be possible to make a key to the edible plants of the British Isles. But there are many thousands of them. Although there are over 20,000 known edible plants worldwide, we eat fewer than 20 of them on a day-to-day basis. But then I don't want you simply to wander through the countryside looking for something to eat. That will never do; just because you can find out that something is edible, it doesn't mean you are going to like it. Moreover, the major reason for this book is not just to describe something as edible – it is to inspire.

I would much rather you decided that you wanted to try something, then went to a safe place to collect it. That way you will develop a great database of knowledge that is your very own.

Happy gathering!

Paul Peacock
Manchester, 2008.

Chapter One
Safe Foraging

This is a very simple book. Its aim is to give the reader a ready resource that allows them to forage for the best wild food and tempts them to go the extra mile in the kitchen and try new things. In order to help with this I would like to introduce a series of rules – some more important than others.

The 10 second rule

If it has been on the floor for less than ten seconds then it's OK to eat. Well, it does depend on what the thing has landed in, or indeed precisley what landed on it before you came along and picked it. Actually, any fool would know the ten-second rule is bogus, but it does illustrate a couple of important principles.

Firstly, we often believe that food is not fit to eat unless it came from a pristine supermarket shelf and has been washed, treated and made sterile. Well, as they say, 'You got'ta eat a lot of dirt before you die.' Wild food is by no means sterile – but on the whole if it is true wild food it is clean.

Secondly, and on the other hand, you must be sure about the environment your food comes from. Urban dogs and cats, riverbank rats, factory pollution, roadside waste (from tyres, that is), dubious ground water, pesticides, human soil (from our bottoms that is – via the drains into the rivers) and a million chemicals that wreck the planet and a lot more besides, can reduce your day's foraging into a vomiting nightmare. The important point is to be sure that what you eat is safe.

The 10 hour rule

If you eat anything raw in the wilderness (for wilderness read clean, unspoiled countryside) then only take a small amount and wait ten hours before trying it in any quantity. If you haven't died in the interim, then carry on, but don't eat more than a small portion. Also, carry a bit with you just in case you start to die on the way home so they can recognise what it is that has killed you – it makes life so much simpler for the coroner.

Seriously though, taking wild food means being careful and moderate; careful in case you do happen to eat some bacterium that doesn't agree with you and also moderate to make sure you do not simply run out there and strip the countryside bare of all its bounty at once. This leads me on to the next rule.

The 10 week rule

Do not return to the same spot to forage for a good long time so that the countryside has plenty of chance to make good what you took. Just because there is a good stand of that delightful wild garlic growing by the river doesn't mean you can go back every time you want to make a garlicky omelette. Give nature time to grow. This is always much more important when foraging for plants than animals. You can go shrimping every day if you lik; replacements should return with each tide, but you couldn't collect seaweed every day – it would all be gone in no time.

Foraging in the countryside

How many stories are there in the UK about poachers? During the time of the Enclosures Act when the ruling classes 'stole by Act of Parliament' common land from the people, there was nowhere left for them to fatten cattle or pigs. Their right to glean the countryside of its bounty disappeared too. We are no longer legally allowed to collect food to eat in most of the countryside in the UK.

This fact has been reinforced by the 'Right to Roam' legislation. You may have the right to wander over large swathes of wild UK, but you do not have the right to pick or eat anything you find. However, so long as you follow the country code, few people in the country will bother you from collecting a few berries or a few mushrooms. And, if you get their permission first, many farmers will be delighted if you help reduce the burden of rabbits or pigeons on their land.

Possibly the most important rule-of-thumb is not to collect everything you see. Be kind to the earth and the earth will be kind to you. What I am about to say is going to get me into trouble. Whenever I talk to birdwatchers about squirrels – the grey ones – I get into a row because city folk (of whom I am one) tend to look at wildlife in the light of their own interest. Many bird, and some mammal lovers too, consider the grey squirrel as a pest to be destroyed. What a waste! This point of view is exactly the same one that brought the squirrels here in the first place! You see, there are lots of people calling for culls of various sorts – usually to remedy some man-made problem or other. The argument is that if we cull the number of grey squirrels then this will give the others a chance to recover their numbers. The same argument goes for magpies (because they eat garden birds), hedgehogs (because they eat birds' eggs on some Scottish island), badgers and goodness knows what.

Well, my motto is never to kill an animal unless you are prepared to do the job yourself or you are prepared to eat it. If you don't like to eat squirrel there are certainly plenty that do, including dogs! So, if you want to kill anything in the countryside, don't prove yourself to be totally barbaric. Use it, honour it and eat it! Foraging is about getting the best from the countryside and as a consequence becoming that bit closer to the ways of the natural world, and that is true whether you simply collect a few berries and mushrooms or kill rabbits and fish or even snails.

The law

You do not need the landowner's permission to pick at a growing plant except for the 180 species listed on Schedule Eight of the Countryside and Wildlife Act 1981, which you will find in the back of this book. But it is against the law to uproot any wild plant – so you can only take a portion of the plant. The other important thing to remember is that wild food should not be taken for financial gain. There are cases where people have been selling wild mushrooms and have been prosecuted for doing so.

Using this book

This handy, practical-sized, book will endeavour to be your guide into foraging. It is not intended to be the ultimate guide to surviving in the wild – you will not find any recipes for catching chickens with a piece of string and a tin of sweetcorn, or how to make a worm curry. But it will help you to know exactly what you can eat. It will tell you what to collect and how to collect it, as well as how to use what you have collected.

Stop wandering haphazardly through the countryside and picking this or that from whatever you find before you. Your journeys for food from the country should be specific. Spend time looking and noticing what is going on around you – look for how wildlife uses the area in which you are foraging and pick up clues about the health of the land around you.

If there is water, does it smell? Is it free flowing? Are any leaves covered in watery silt or slime? Are there many animals about on the land? Are there a lot of faeces on the floor? Is there any evidence of dogs and cats? Can you smell urine? Are there lots of nettles around?

Once you find a supply of food you would like to reap, you will need to make sure you can take it legally. Then you will need to be sure you can take it safely, and then if the food is safe in itself, and this is where this book will help you.

Our plant key will provide you with a simple and easy to understand guide to wild food. It will tell you how poisonous a particular plant is, and then will give instructions on how to cook a number of them.

The definition of culture

I strongly believe that culture is what makes life bearable. And, regardless how you might try to argue to the contrary, nothing makes life more bearable than a fruit flan of wild berries washed down by a glass of fruit wine made from the same berries. It's not just the consumption, it's the making, the collecting and, possibly more than anything, it's the sharing.

And you will find wine recipes. Fruit wine, sap wine and elderflower wine; all wonderful, bottled sunshine!

If only...

Oh if only gentlemen could wear britches and frock coats, tricorn hats and very gaudy waistcoats and walk with a stick and pass the time of day in a pleasant manner! Well, I can wish for more reasons than just an admiration for strange and eccentric fashion. When men swapped colour for black and brown they also, coincidentally, started to pollute the land. Before the industrial revolution you could expect the good earth to nourish you without problem. Then, just twenty years of wearing black and you were hard pushed to find a clean river in the whole of the United Kingdom.

In 1770 The Medlock River which flows into the Irwell and then into the Mersey, was full of salmon and trout. The local people who fished in it ran the risk of terrible punishments from the very harsh magistrates who somehow believed the rivers and fish belonged solely to them. By the end of the century the local farmers and peasants were nudged off the land by Act of Parliament and the river lost all its life. The reason for this was a factory making lime, then another to be built later making chemicals and then explosives, and the importation of the greatest concentration of pigs on the planet. This change came when people realised they could make money from the land instead of a mere living.

The Medlock officially remained the dirtiest river in the world for over 150 years. Once you could eat the fruit that grew on its banks but this hasn't happened in living memory. The soil is absolutely laden with heavy metals and, to add insult to injury, the spoil of sixty years of coal burning at the local power station along with the out-fall of a sewage treatment works, has continued to seep into the river and pollute its valley.
But this landscape can revert. Over-planted slag-heaps will be laden with heavy metals for a long time to come, but if you take away the sources of pollution,

the processes of nature will reclaim the land again. Since money is no longer made in the valley from pigs, hundreds of tonnes of effluent no longer flow into the river. The oxygenating fresh water clears away the effluent and bacteria in the soil begin to break down generations of slurry. Young birch and shrubs make room for fungi and new fruit trees appear, often escapees from gardens. Tomatoes from the soil of the treatment works spring up on the banks of the river and brambles overgrow the spaces between the fields of green covered slag. In time even this most industrial corner of the first ever industrial city in the world will be clean enough for people to eat the natural fruit of the sun on the land.

And so to this book. It is an empowering feeling to collect berries or mushrooms and feed yourself. I repeat, this is no survival manual, more a guide to getting close to the land that feeds us and understanding some of the plants therein. Even small children once had an almost encyclopaedic understanding of which plant could be eaten and which to avoid and of how the plants grew and even some of their folklore. Even my own generation, now sadly wandering close to the exit on the great motorway of life, used to sing about wild plants both in school and at home. Maybe our greatest legacy could be to bring some of these old songs and old ways back into mainstream use? Who knows?

What? Where?

There is always something to eat in every season, and plenty of it. When you add to the list those plants we ought to know such as flowering cherry, apple, vegetables and the grasses that come and go, you get a picture of the seasonality of the climate in the UK.

Certainly farm workers of a hundred years ago would know, and indeed be waiting for, the times when various plants came into use. Similarly, long awaited medicine stocks would be filled and replenished at the right time of the year and, whereas people always grew a large amount of their own food, the natural bounty of life was there to improve and embellish it.

The simple cycle of life, once so richly embedded in all people, seems to be all but ignored in our country through lack of use. The longed for 'self-sufficiency' movement seem bent on growing their own and keeping livestock, but a good 25% of the common peasant's health and food came from the wild. So hopefully people will learn in the future to do more than simply growing and tending and caring for their own at the expense of others. Or worse still, exchanging eight hours a day for just enough money to buy food gathered from everywhere on the planet.

Feeding yourself is an act of grace and a link with the planet that created a bounty for you to share. How much better is that grace when you share in the seasons and processes that created that bounty? For you to know how to make a salt alternative, or how to chew a leaf to slake your thirst on a hot day and, of course, which leaf to chew in the first place! How to make tea that relieves your toothache, and how to find food when nothing else is growing.

A knowledge of how the seasons bring their bounty also brings hope. There is always something coming in a few weeks and the wait is seasoned with preparation.

Winter	Spring
Sea beet	Wild garlic
Sea purslane	Garlic mustard
Mushrooms	Sea kale
Frost softened rosehips	Sea beet
Bittercress	Watercress
Dandelion leaves	Fat hen
Chickweed	Morels
Primroses	Lime leaves
Alexanders	Nettles
Wood sorrel	Dandelions
	Chickweed
	Hawthorn leaves
	Elderflower
	Sea lettuce
Summer	**Autumn**
Lime flowers	Nettles
Samphire	Elderberries
Sea purslane	Mushrooms galore
Sea beet	Apples
Sea lettuce	Hawberries
Green walnuts	Sloes
Chamomile	Chestnuts
Blackberries	Walnuts
Ceps	Cobnuts
Chanterelles	Chestnuts
Blackberries	
Wild cherries	
Apples	
Sorrell	

Chapter Two
Herbaceous Plants

These plants are all soft bodied. The word herbaceous means non-woody, but then botany gets all complicated and hot under the collar. These twenty five plants are not easily mistaken for anything else and are useful in the kitchen, the home in general or the beer tent.

The majority of them are easily found while walking around parks and woodlands, on hills and by rivers. I make no apology for excluding perfectly good plants such as wild chervil which is a fantastic alternative to parsnip, but is so easily mistaken for hemlock. You don't want to follow Socrates to the grave, however clever he was!

Please only collect just enough of these plants. You are not alone in the world and there are plenty of wild creatures who want their share and you are not cooking for the army. And please, watch what you do with your feet. Don't trample the world to death. As someone said, tread lightly in the earth.

Most of these plants are easily identified from the spring through to the onset of autumn. All keep well in the freezer or fridge and all make really good eating.

Enjoy!

Bistort

Polygonum bistorta

You can recognise the bistort by the flower stripe which grows vertically away from the mass of leaves and is tipped with pink and white flowers that are so small and tightly packed it looks as though the stick was dipped in some candy.

The leaves, though simple, resemble dock leaves. They are about 25 – 30cm long and look like the ends of African paddles. The leaves are edible, and have a slightly acidic flavour. They do have oxalic acid in them, so you should avoid eating them if you have rheumatism, but they are quite safe in most cases. The plant is collected to make a bitter pudding called Easter Ledger, though I doubt it has been made in many a year.

Easter Ledger

A handful each of finely chopped bistort, nettle and dandelion leaves and blackcurrant
Two handfuls of oatmeal
One finely chopped large onion
1 egg

Combine all the ingredients except the egg in a bowl and soak in water overnight. Drain in the morning and put into a greased baking dish. Cook for an hour at 180°C and then transfer the hot contents to a bowl. Break the egg into the mixture and stir it in to cook the egg in the residual heat. Season to taste.

Alternatively, you could simply chop up bistort and nettle leaves and throw them into an omelette!

Bramble

When God threw Satan out of Heaven, it is said that he fell into a pile of brambles. This took place on Old St. Michael's Day, which was the 10th October. This date saw the end of the war in heaven, with St. Michael winning, of course. In 1752 the government passed the New Calendar Act, and Michaelmas became the 29th September. The importance of this for bramble collectors is that you are not supposed to pick the fruit after Old Michaelmas because the Devil is said to spit on them on that day. It is true that by mid-October they are almost not worth eating as the fruit that remains is poor in quality, low in sugar and ferments easily.

In some parts of the country the Devil urinates on the brambles, and in other places even worse. So watch out what you eat! In truth, a number of insects feed on brambles, and their saliva does digest the fruit from the outside, making them mushy.

Brambles are often found in cemeteries. In Georgian times and earlier they were planted over graves to stop the dead from walking. Some of the plants that are found in churchyards are over 200 years old!

We owe much of our language to brambles. Being 'dragged through a hedge backwards' was a common cure. Pulling a person through a bramble bush is said to cure many ailments. However, if it had happened to me I, for one, would pretend to have gotten well too!

Botany
Brambles are members of the rose family (rosaceae) so they have five petals, usually whitish pink to pink. They

look almost like miniature roses, apple or buttercup flowers. Each flower is backed by a set of five sepals which are hard, green leaflets whose function is to protect the flower bud.

The flowers appear on canes that are older than one season, and these can be very long indeed, sometimes in excess of six to eight feet. Each cane, or stem, is covered with hard, wooded thorns and the whole plant grows as a thicket.

Brambles suffer from viral diseases. One common defence to this in plants is genetic variation. Consequently, there is a huge amount of inter-breeding within the bramble family and they form new varieties very easily, often crossing with nearby strains. They also have a trick which allows them to produce genetically different offspring. This is called changing ploidy. That is to say they can produce seeds that have double, quadruple or sometimes half the number of chromosomes in their cells.

Consequently, the botany of this plant is very complex indeed.

How to collect
If you simply thrust your hand into the bush to get at the berries they will get very badly cut and scratched. If you wear gloves they will forever get on your nerves as the catch on the thorns. What you need is a long pole made from wood with a hook on the end. A nail set at a backwards angle will do. Then you can pull the cane out of the way of the others and pick off the fruit. This also allows you to pick the highest fruit – you frequently see them very high indeed.

When you collect the fruit, put your fingers behind the berries and pull them off the plant. They should leave the conical bed behind. If not they are under ripe but if they fall apart when you touch them, then they are over ripe.

For pies, wines and cordials you only need the full dupelets; that is the little round, full, juice laden parts of the berry. All the rest will add bitterness to the fruit. To collect a bucket full will take many hours. It is slow, backbreaking work, but is well worth it in the end.

Medicinal uses
Apart from being dragged through a hedge backwards, brambles have long been used for medicinal purposes.

Sore throats
Boil some bramble leaves in water and gargle. This is also good for sore gums. It works by acting as an astringent and shrinking the tissues.

Anti-fungal
The same liquid can be used alongside conventional treatments for thrush, but do not give it to infants or children.

Tonic
The juice from blackberries and raspberries is a pleasant tonic, particularly when taken just ripe. Boil the fruit with double the amount of water, squashing them with a spoon. Strain and leave to cool and then refrigerate. Serve with a big spoon of honey. The complex sugars in this drink will aid recovery. It is said to be particularly helpful for people recovering from shingles. Be careful taking this during pregnancy as raspberry has been

linked to promoting contractions of the uterus.

Non-food use
They have many other uses too, including splitting the vines to make really good twine once the hooks have been removed. It was used past times in the brush and basket industry.

Dye manufacture
Considering the stain left by brambles on your fingers it wouldn't be a surprise to learn that you can dye cloth with them. You need to collect as many berries as you can and then double the volume with water. This mixture is mashed to release the cell contents and then boiled for a couple of hours, stirring from time to time.

The liquor is strained through muslin into a plastic bucket and a fixative is added. This can be as simple as half a cup of salt dissolved in four times its volume of water. Potash alum is a better fixative, used at the same dilution.

A better dye is obtained by boiling bramble roots in the same proportions. This gives a dye that is variable in shade from yellow to orange, depending on the plant and the fixative. This time it has to be acidic, so a cup of vinegar is added to half a gallon of dye.

You can use the remaining root fibres and beat them with a hammer to macerate them and then lay the pulp into water and make paper.

Fencing and hedging
Brambles are a favourite hedge starter since they grow quickly and create an inpenetrable mass, keeping

livestock at bay and protecting young shoots that are growing through to create the hedge.

Bramble Jelly

1.5kg brambles
3 large under ripe cooking apples cored and chopped
500ml water
An excess of granulated sugar – see method

The apple is in the recipe to increase the pectin content. You can make your own liquid pectin by boiling a lot of chopped, under ripe apples in twice their weight of water until it has reduced by half. Strain and use this in jam making.

Put all the ingredients into a heavy based saucepan and bring to the boil. Turn down the heat and simmer for 20-25 minutes. The fruit should be completely smooth and soft. Tip the fruit and juice into the jelly bag or muslin and allow the liquid to drip through until everything is released.

You need to measure the sugar. For every 500ml liquid you need 500g sugar.

Return the juice and sugar back into the now clean preserving pan and heat over a low heat until all the sugar has dissolved. Boil the liquid for around 15 minutes and check for the setting point. You do this by putting a teaspoon of the liquid onto a cold plate and, when cool, push your finger through it. If the gap remains then the jelly is ready for setting. If it falls back, continue to boil. Repeat this cycle of testing/boiling until you get a setting point.

Remove any scum in the pan and fill the jam jars to the

top. Cover with a greaseproof disc and close the lid while still hot. Do not forget to label with the date.

Apple & Blackberry Crumble

Four large cooking apples (peeled and cored)
400g blackberries
4 level tablespoons granulated sugar

For the Crumble:

200g flour
100g oats
200g butter
200g demerara sugar

Slice or cube the apples and mix all the ingredients in a large dish.

Rub the flour, oats and butter together to a crumbly texture. Loosely combine with the sugar. Pour evenly over the fruit.

Bake in a hot oven at 175°C for around 30 minutes.

Bramble Wine

1kg blackberries (more if possible)
500g sugar
Juice of two lemons
Teaspoon brewers yeast

You will need:
A sterile bucket
Large sheets of muslin
A large pan
A demijohn and airlock

Sterilise everything. Put the fruit in a sterile bucket and pour the same volume of boiling water over the fruit. Mash (I use a rolling pin) the fruit to release the juices.

Strain the liquid into a gallon stock pan and bring to the boil. Add the sugar and stir until it has dissolved. Allow the liquid to cool and then strain into the demijohn. Add the yeast and airlock.

When it stops bubbling you can rack off the wine repeatedly into clean demijohns, allowing the lees to settle each time.

Broom
Cytisus ssp.

It is said that kissing is in season whenever the broom is in flower. You cannot mistake this plant because it has bright yellow complicated flowers and spiky stems. The late John Seymour was partial to broom wine and in his final years was too blind to pick the flowers without impaling his fingers on the thorns. You have to be careful.

Of course the plant is in flower all year long, so there is no excuse for missing out on a quick kiss!

Before the rose, this plant was the emblem of the English Kings. Its medieval name, *Planta Genista,* and the family of Kings from Henry II to Richard III (14 of them, in fact) were all known as the Plantagenet kings.

Broom Tea

Collect your broom flowers and keep them away from plastic. A tea caddy is a good storage place, but you can

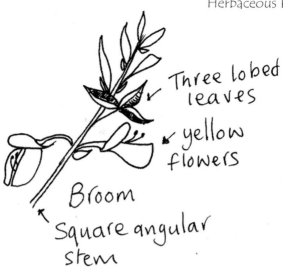

Three lobed leaves

yellow flowers

Broom

Square angular stem

also freeze them. Simply take a tablespoon full of them, put them in a cup (an infuser is even better) and pour boiling water over them. A spoon of honey will add flavour and sweetness.

Broom wine

About a kilo of broom flowers in a large pan (That's a lot of flowers!) is boiled with 500g raisins and the juice of three oranges. Once steeped (brought to the boil and then allowed to cool), give the contents of the pan a good mashing. Strain into another pan and dissolve 500g of sugar per litre of juice. Set into a fermentation vessel with a teaspoon full of yeast.

Rack in the normal way and bottle. The longer you can leave it the better.

Bugle
Ajuga reptans

Its other name, stitchwort, gives some idea about its

blood clotting and skin healing properties

This is a member of the labiate, or dead nettle family. The plant is recognised by the spike of blue flowers that grow from leaves that look like nettle leaves but have no sting. They actually make excellent garden plants and are found on the edges of woodland, where there is dappled shade and the soil is slightly damp.

It was used as a treatment for stopping blood flow, particularly when the patient had TB or consumption and was spitting blood. But it only stopped the blood flow, not the disease. It helps the skin to heal and concoctions are made from the whole plant. Simply steep the top of the plant in boiling water and use the cooled, strained liquid as a gargle.

The leaves and the flowers can be used in salads and are really pleasant too!

Burdock
Arctium lappa

Wherever there is nettle growing, you will find burdock. It is a little like sorrel, but the leaves are rounder, thick and not pointed. There are the same spikes of flowers, but they are bigger and borne like thistles. There are plenty of thick stems. A relative, the fiddle dock, has leaves that look like violins. The burdock does have something of the fiddle about the leaf.

The fruits are covered in spines and have hooked ends so that the fruit is carried about attached to the fur of passing animals. It is particularly effective on wooly coats!

The hairs around the seeds are poisonous and, since they are small, they have a tendency to get in the nose and lungs, probably the worst place to ingest a poison.

You will find this plant wherever the soil is disturbed or at the woodland edge. It grows well on any soil type and is remarkably good at growing in all conditions from arid sand to muddy clay.

You can use the leaves which are a little thick and unpalatable (well, I don't like them) but they are not too bad when parboiled. They are best when the stems and veins are removed. When lightly boiled they have a flavour that is reminiscent of asparagus, and they also make an excellent alternative to spinach.

The roots can be eaten too. Choose only the thinner, young roots that do not have a woody stem. They are excellent washed and boiled. They take on the flavour of whatever they are cooked with. There is a good deal of inulin in them, a double starch that cannot be digested by humans, but in some people they can ferment. In these cases the meal can be followed by a good deal of wind.

Dandelion and Burdock

You need dandelion roots and burdock roots in equal quantities, 200g of each. Cut them into 2cm pieces and dry them in a very low oven.

When they are dried out, bash them about in a pestle and mortar.

Add to 2 litres of boiling water along with the juice of

two oranges and their grated peel. Do not add the pits at all; they are bitter.

Boil for around 30 minutes and then strain through a double layer of muslin. Return to the heat and then stir in 1kg of sugar until it is dissolved. Transfer to sterile bottles. If you are not careful, airborne yeast can get in and spoil the drink, so it won't keep forever. Alternatively you can transfer to a demijohn and add some brewer's yeast. (I think I prefer it this way!)

Chickweed
Stellaria media

The chickweed is a bit of a pest in the garden, especially in lawns where it grows rapidly. It looks like a long string of leaves on a straggling stem. At the end, and sometimes in the middle of the long trailing or ground covering stems are borne little yellow and white flowers that look like stars, hence the name Stellaria.

The leaves look like archetypal tea leaves, though they are not as leathery, and are about 1cm long. It grows in profusion and has been traditionally fed to young birds, hence the name chickweed.

small white flowers

Long brown stems

chickweed

The juice of chickweed in some boiling water and allowed to cool has long been used as an eye wash, a job at which it has been particularly efficient. Borne in pairs on the stem, the leaves are an excellent substitute for cress. In fact I think it is much better than cress.

The stems do get in your teeth, so make sure you only use the leaves which are best stripped of the delicate stems with a fork. You can cook the leaves in soups, or simply add them to salads.

Crab apple
Malus sylvestris

The European wild apple is overlooked these days. Why eat sour crab apples when you can go to the supermarket and eat real ones?

The plant is small, around 3–4 feet tall and densely twiggy. The 'apples' are small and yellow in colour and borne together in groups. The word crab means small and bitter, and the Old English word crabby is used to refer to someone being bitter and annoying.

The fruit of the crab apple is very tart and needs plenty of sugar to be palatable, but makes the best jelly there is because of its very high pectin content.

The flowers look just like apple tree flowers but the leaves are larger and the fruit smaller. They look like small, misshapen apples and are unmistakable.

Crab Apple Jelly

Collect a few kilos of crab apples and remove the leaves and twigs. Cover with water and boil them for 30 – 45 minutes until the apples become soft enough to pulp. Remove from the heat and, when the liquid is cool enough, give the apples a good mash.

Strain the juice through a jelly bag into a second pan. For every litre of juice add 500g sugar, stirring until dissolved. You can add a large knob of butter to reduce the foaming, which should be scraped off.

Boil this until you get a setting point, and pour into hot, sterile jars.

Cuckoo pint

Arum maculatum

Treat this with respect as the berries are poisonous and the plant has an unpleasant smell. Once upon a time the Cuckoo pint, also known as Jack in the Pulpit, Lords and Laries and the more telling Starch Root, was dug up and the roots used for food. The roots have a 25% starch content making them a perfectly acceptable vegetable. But the whole plant contains Oxalic acid and must be cooked fully in order to remove the poison. If you eat it raw it is very unpleasant, something similar to having needles pushed into your tongue and you must handle the roots carefully as they can cause chapping. Once cooked this is no longer a problem and, if you have the odd ruff hanging around waiting to be startched, then here's your solution.

The leaves look like the points of spears and the yellowish-white flower looks like a spike tucked in a whitish green leaf. It is worth repeating that the berries are highly poisonous and it is the root that is used for food. This does create a problem because of the legal consequences of uprooting a wild plant.

To cook the root, wash and cut it into manageable pieces and roast them. If you are going to grind the root for flour you will need to roast it dry at 150°C for an hour and then leave it to dry. This high starch flour was once known as Portland Sago. The dried roots, bashed with a hammer to break the tissues, make a tea with boiling water called salop.

If you are going to eat the root with a meal, splash it with a little oil and cook it at 200°C for 30 minutes.

There are a number of preparations of the same name, some using orchid roots, others using combinations of Cockoo Pint and other roots. It was once considered to be an aphrodisiac and was the common tea before the world started to drink the leaves of the camellia from China and India.

The leaves can be taken, but have toxic problems and have to be cooked for a very long time, preferably in several changes of water, so it is no longer really used.

Dandelion leaves
Taraxacum officinallis

There is a tale of a schoolboy mixing his history and French and writing in his book, "Richard of England, dent de lion!" How much the old king would have appreciated being called lion's tooth I don't know, but it explains nicely how we get the name dandelion, after the shape of its leaves, which look like lion's teeth.

Dandelion is also known as bitterwort, mostly because of the sharpness of its roots.

The origins of this plant are somewhat mysterious. It was a cultivated vegetable for many years and only fell out of favour after the nineteenth century. It was mostly grown for smoking. It was common practice to cure the leaves like tobacco and then smoke them in clay pipes as a replacement for the more expensive tobacco. The dandelion went out of favour as the Empire increased and tobacco, which was much preferred, became affordable.

I knew a chap once who cured dandelion in the 1970's. "I've smoked 'em since I was eight years old!" he said. He was well over eighty when he died, but he had never, in all his years of smoking dandelion leaves in a little pipe which looked at least as old as he did, had a day's illness. Well, that's what he told me!

Botany
The scientific name, *Taraxacum officinalis* is Greek and translates as 'official cure for disorders.' It is really a member of the aster family, related to the Camomile and the Ox-eye daisy, the Osteospermums and the Marguerites. As any gardener will tell you they have extensive root systems. The leaves are heavily toothed (hence the name) and the inflorescence (flower stalk) is simple and tubular.

Health benefits
Dandelions are well known as a remedy for kidney disorders. However, if you are having pains in the small of the back, and on passing urine, you really should see a doctor first.

It promotes the passing of water, hence another name for the plant is piss-en-lit, or wet-the-bed. Because it stimulates the production of urine it has also been used to purify blood and clear gout, which is the collection of uric acid crystals in the joints of the feet.

Further health benefits of dandelions are said to include reduced blood pressure, but again you would do well not to treat yourself with regard to this.

Food

Related to chicory, dandelion can be quite bitter. This can be overcome in two ways. Firstly, you can collect only the new leaves, which are much sweeter. Secondly, you can put a flowerpot over the plant to keep the light out. This blanches it and creates a milder flavour.

Dandelion leaves are most frequently used with lettuce, rocket, nasturtium and any other leaves you may have to hand to make a mixed salad. Only one in ten of the leaves should be dandelion or you'll be running to the toilet all day.

Savoury

This is a peasant's dish of fried green stuff. Combined with nettles in equal quantities, boiled first; they resemble spinach. However, this can then be wrung out to remove as much water as possible and then fried in bacon fat or blended with a little cream for a tasty spring meal.

The dandelion is an important plant for the so-called hungry gap, when much of the autumn crops are used up and the first crops of the spring have not yet appeared. This is the gap when traditionally food is, at best, basic. It coincides, more or less, with Lent, a time of reserve and fasting which is just as well really. Currently we do not experience a hungry gap, but it's good to know about dandelions just the same. They are an excellent source of vitamins and really do improve the health of people who eat them in the spring.

A big problem is that the plant is attractive to cats. Actually, perhaps I should say, they smell (to cats that is) like a good old tom cat so wherever they grow in the city you can be sure that some cat or other has sprayed on it. If you are collecting dandelion leaves, give them a very good wash first.

Dandelion flowers

Collecting the bright flowers is beneficial because, if they set seed, there will be hundreds more dandelions! The flowers are compound, each head having dozens of little florets. Known as poor man's saffron you can get the orange dye out of them. Being quite edible, they make food, especially rice, quite pretty. Just mix a few of the florets (not the whole head!) in with the rice.

The best use for dandelion flowers, in my opinion, of course, is the making of wine.

Midday Dandelion wine

This wine gets its name from the fact that the flowers are collected at midday when they are fully open. You need to pull the florets off the green haul.

1kg dandelion flowers
1kg sugar
4 oranges
5 litres water
yeast

Set the water boiling in a stockpot and remove the florets from the plants. Add them to the boiling water. Leave the leaves to steep for 24 hours as the water cools.

Peel the oranges and remove as much of the pith as you can. Chop the peel into small pieces and add to the pot. Juice the oranges and add this too. Bring the liquid back to the boil and simmer for 30 minutes.

Allow to cool completely and then strain into a second pan or a bucket. Dissolve the sugar in boiling water and mix with the juice. Pour into a demijohn and then a teaspoon of yeast will set it going. Close with an air-lock.

When it stops bubbling, rack into a clean demijohn and repeat each month for two months. After six months it should be quite a robust wine. You can bottle it after the second racking.

Dandelion sweet and savoury

You can add red cabbage to this if you like. Experimentation is the name of the game. It is particularly good with red wine and beef stock, which is then eaten with venison

5 handfuls of young washed dandelion leaves
3 decent sized shallots
1 handful of raisins
1 glass of white wine or stock

Shred the dandelion leaves, finely chop the shallots and caramelise in a little oil on a very low light. Add the dandelion to the shallots and add the white wine or stock. Cook until the leaves are soft and the liquid has reduced by ¾. Finally, add the raisins and cook for 5 mins on a low light

Dandelion and Burdock

Dandelion and Burdock is one of those drinks that is commonly bought, but few know how to make. There are lots of recipes out there and ours is called beer. Nettle beer was very popular for many. In fact it should be called nettle ale, since beer is a drink made from hops.

Burdock is the ideal plant to blend with dandelion because it compliments some of the bitterness. The recipe is an ancient one and was a way of making the very best use of the farmyard. Nettles, docks and dandelions grow best of all where animals have urinated. You can use this knowledge to tell where the animals in fields like to congregate. The nitrates which form in the soil are ideal minerals for growing many plants.

Dandelion and burdock ale

This drink needs plenty of sweetness to work, and I prefer to make it with honey. You get a much richer flavour than with pure sugar. The more honey you have, the better the drink. What you have to beware of is steeping the leaves too much. Some old recipes call for burdock leaves and root to be steeped for days. Those of you who have made comfrey tea in a pillowcase plunged into a barrel of water will realise that the smell is somewhat off-putting.

500g young nettle leaves
200g young dandelion leaves
200g burdock leaves
200g burdock roots, shredded
1kg honey
Juice of 5 lemons
5 litres of water
Yeast

Place the leaves and roots into the pan, add the water straight from the kettle and bring to the boil. Simmer for 30 minutes and then sieve all the spent ingredients.

Pour the lot into a large, sterilised fermentation bin and stir in the honey and the lemon juice. When the liquid has cooled but is still luke warm, sprinkle over 1 tablespoon of brewers yeast and cover the vessel for a week.

Siphon the beer into sealable, sterile bottles and add a spoonful of sugar to each bottle. This causes a secondary fermentation to add the extra fizz. If you can, leave the bottles on a stone floor to allow the sediment to fall. If you simply put them onto floorboards, the vibrations in the house will not allow the spent yeast to settle.

After about a week or two you can start to drink the beer. It is not all that alcoholic, and in medieval times children would drink it along with adults.

Fat Hen
Chenopodium album

Fat hen looks like an unmade bed when you come across it. It has leaves that are very loosely serrated, but some not at all. The best they can be described as is lobed. Some of the leaves are long and thin, others short and more rounded. The colour is as though you got some dark green and mixed in some cream, and underneath the leaves it is slightly lighter.

The flowers, which look as though they were grassy, or like millet fed to caged birds, are lighter green and lie in bunches from the axils of the leaf branches. The stem is angular and light green in colour. The leaves are cooked and eaten like spinach. There have been some worries about the high nitrate content of this plant, and consequently it is likely best used as a compost material. However, the leaves are tasty and do make an ideal alternative to cabbage.

As you would imagine, hens do well on it too.

Garlic mustard (Jack-by-the-hedge)
Alliaria petiolata

Very common in hedges, this plant smells of garlic and has very tasty leaves. The leaves are heart shaped and serrated. The flowers are small and white.

It is a member of the cruciferae, which is characterised by four petals in the shape of a cross. The early botanists named the whole group for religious reasons.

Its flavour is a combination of garlic and mustard and it has plenty of uses in the kitchen. It can be added to salads on hot days and stews on cold ones. The leaves can be frozen and then simply added as a seasoning to savoury pies and other dishes.

The major importance of this plant is that the young leaves are available in January, making this an excellent plant for the hungry gap.

One warning: the mustard flavour comes from sulphur based molecules, which for me at least, causes very major exhaust problems shared by all the family.

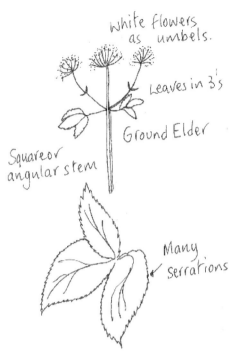

white flowers as umbels.

Leaves in 3's

Ground Elder

Square or angular stem

Many serrations

Ground Elder
Aegopodium podagraria

You can blame the church for this amazing plant. In many parts of the country it is illegal to allow this plant to grow, which is odd because it is perfectly edible, and is in fact quite pleasant.

The story goes that St. Gerard sent some monks this plant because they were praying about the trouble they all had from gout. My remedy would have been a few months of abstinence, but then I'm not a saint. Anyway, the herb is also known as gout weed and Bishop's weed. Indeed, the scientific name, *Aegopodium* means gout in the foot. As you would have thought, the plant does help in cases of gout.

Description

What you see is a mass of leaves borne on the end of stalks that look like very thin rhubarb stems, but are completely green. The leaves are rounded at the stem end and more pointed at the other, and lightly serrated. They have flowers that are borne on umbels.

Collect the leaves and use them the same day. They will boil down like spinach. Because of this you can also put them in soups, but experiment with them. Some people love the flavour, others hate it. It seems to be a genetic choice, so you might just find it difficult to get along with.

Hairy Bittercress
Cardamine hirsuta

This plant grows all over the country on waste ground, at all heights and in all climates. It is a short, acid green looking plant with little penny round leaves borne in threes, fives and sevens on little stems that come from a central point. It has little flowers that burst out of the centre of the plant and in all it looks rather like a very untidy herb.

The flowers are small, white and appear on the end of a stem that will also have the fruits developing at the same time as the flowers. The fruits look like thickened match stalks on the end of the stem.

The whole plant is edible. It is a peppery herb that you can use instead of cress, and makes a piquant sandwich for those who like it hot.

Heather
Calluna vulgaris

This plant has been used for all sorts of reasons over the years. Children used to hollow out the roots and make whistles from them and the leaves and stems have been used as roofing material, thatching, bedding for animals and mattress stuffing for humans. The flowers have been used as an antiseptic for many years and a tea made from the branches is said to be very good for urinary infections.

The stems and leaves can be used in the brewing of ale, and this is the very best use for the plant, although the flowers, drizzled over salads, are quite nice too! (Note that beer is not beer unless it has hops in it, so the correct word for this is ale.)

Heather ale

This is enough to make 40 litres, but I don't have a pan big enough to boil it all, so I make my wort separately and then dilute it to 40 litres in my fermentation vessel.

2.5kg pale ale malt
750g dextrine malt
200g roast barley
300g heather tops (tops of the shoots)

Once boiling, turn the heat right down and leave it just below a simmer for an hour. Strain through a muslin and then bring to 40 litres with cold water. When completely cool, add the yeast and ferment. I use a pressure vessel from which I can pour straight into bottles.

Horseradish
Armoracia rusticana

What a great plant this is! Its knotted roots are used to make hot sauce and to put hair on sailors' chests. (Honest!)

You will find it on any well drained soil, almost anywhere. It tends to grow in great clumps. Please bear in mind that it is illegal to uproot any wild plant. But a bit of root every now and again? And who knows, by the time you are reading this the law might have changed?

Medically speaking, the oils from horseradish are antibiotic and have been used for a long time as an antiseptic, especially on cuts. However, much better preparations made from garlic are available that make this plant redundant. It is a rich source of sulphonomide molecules which have all sorts of important health benefits, but they are in a form that is far too difficult for humans to take.

One side effect of horseradish (well I blame it anyway) is extremely pungent flatulence. A tea made from horseradish roots boiled together makes an excellent natural anti-fungal treatment against botrytis in the greenhouse and orchard. However, I have to point out that it is illegal to make your own pesticides and fungicides.

Description
The plant looks like a cross between a lettuce and a stepmother's tongue. The leaves are borne on little stalks that come directly out of the ground and are about 30cm long. They come to a point and sometimes

they are wrinkled and sometimes not. It is as though someone had pulled a romaine lettuce apart and planted the leaves.

Beneath the ground they are a mass of roots. You should collect a fat piece, probably no bigger than a 10p piece in thickness. You can grate this. Please remember to wash your hands before you go to the toilet when collecting this plant!

You can use the leaves in a salad, but only one or two of them. You can also sprout the seeds to make an interesting addition to the salad bowl.

Horseradish sauce

This is Mrs Beeton's recipe, but I think she made it a bit too strong to feed to her wayward husband.

Grate 40g horseradish and mix it well with 5g caster sugar, 5g salt, 2.5g pepper and 5g mustard. Moisten it with sufficient vinegar to give it the consistency of cream, and serve in a tureen. You can cool this off and very much improve the appearance and flavour by adding 25ml of cream.

To heat it to serve with hot roast beef, put it in a bain marie or a jar, then place in a saucepan of boiling water; make it hot, but do not allow it to boil or it will curdle.

Lady's mantle
Alchemilla mollis

This is one of the herbs that Cromwell knocked about a bit. It used to be known as Our Lady's mantle due to the shape of the leaves looking a little like a shawl. But the Puritans changed its name at about the same time they cancelled Christmas.

The whole plant is covered with hairs, which means that rainfall collects on the leaves, resembling jewels. For this reason the water was collected as it was supposed to have magical properties and for centuries it was known as celestial water.

The plant itself is quite edible, but has a bitter, sharp flavour. To add to its religious background, a Lenten pudding called Easter ledger used to be eaten on Good Friday. The leaves can be used in salads and the root is eaten, boiled.

The leaves of Lady's mantle are drunk by everyone who enjoys ordinary tea since the dried leaves are used in its blending.

Herb Lady's tea

An infusion of a single leaf of Lady's mantle, nettle, mint and lemon balm makes for an excellent brew. Just pour two cups of boiling water over them in a tea pot and leave the mixture to cool. You can add a little more flavour with lemon and honey. An excellent, relaxing drink.

Mint
Mentha ssp.

Mint is really the same as nettles, except they have no sting and have a minty taste. The leaves of all mints are acidic green and serrated. The flowers are borne in pairs on either side of the stem at different heights on the plant.

Of course the plant is most easily recognised by its smell and is extremely versatile.

There are about 40 different kinds of mint in the UK, not all Mentha species, and not all wild. Everything from chocolate mint to pineapple mint has been produced because the plant hybridises so easily. In the wild you are more likely to find garden escapees.

Apart from being minty and extremely useful in the kitchen, mint is one of the most health giving plants there is, up there with the likes of garlic and onion. In this case it is the digestive system that benefits. When certain bacteria enter our system, we respond by producing nitric oxide to kill them, and this can cause us severe problems. Mint aids the digestive system fight bacteria as well as easing the membranes that so easily become inflamed.

A few sprigs of mint in hot water produces a calming drink, and provides a clue to the next benefit we get from the plant; menthol oils. The smell of mint has two very definite effects: As well as a very definite calming effect on the digestive system, it also restricts the blood flow in the capillaries of the sinus, thus leaving more space for the airways. The result is a temporary improvement in breathing.

The second benefit is the effect it has on the brain. We get a very strong emotional response from mint. For most people it is a calming restorative, giving a sense of well-being.

Mint sauce

This is really a herbal vinegar, and you can choose, should you make your own, the type of vinegar you use instead of that industrial stuff that we buy from the shops. White wine vinegar makes a good choice or try a mixture of 3 parts white vinegar to one part rose water.

200g finely chopped fresh mint leaves
200ml malt vinegar
50g or 3 tablespoons white sugar

It is best to make this fresh each time. It is just an infusion. Chop up the mint as finely as possible and mix the rest together. But you can bottle or even freeze it.

If you replace the vinegar with sugar syrup or a mixture of honey and water in equal quantities then you will have some fantastic mint ice cubes for Pimms type summer drinks (Oh! Roll on hot weather!)

Mint paste

This is a basic sweet paste with which you can make any number of biscuits, ice creams and sweets. You can replace the nuts with digestive biscuits if you like. You need to use the food processor and it takes forever to clean, but it is well worth it.

Use equal quantities by weight of mint, honey and macadamia nuts or biscuits. Simply whizz them through the food processor and scrape them out.

You can mix these with oats to make mint flapjacks, or fold into flour (it takes a whole lifetime so you might not bother) and add some butter to form a dough and make biscuits.

Raita

This is a condiment used in Indian cuisine. It is simple to make and very cooling.

50g chopped mint
200ml yoghurt (plain – not strawberry!)
100g finely diced cucumber

Simply combine and place in the fridge for a couple of hours before serving. You might need a tiny dash of salt.

Nettle
Urtica dioica

The Nettle is an ancient plant which shares its history with our own agricultural development from the late Stone age. Consequently we have found many uses for this very versatile plant.

Botany
Nettles are a member of a huge group of plants known as the labiata – or lipped plants. Not all of them sting, but the common nettle *Urtica dioica* does. The nettle sting is full of the irritants *acetyl choline* and *histamine*.

The plant is rich in nutrients and grows best where animals have urinated, particularly sheep and cattle. Although the soil might have a strong smell, the nettle is still fit to eat.

The leaf is spade shaped and highly serrated. They are borne in pairs or groups at nodes along the stem and the flowers, which look like wild hops, are found at intervals in the leaf axils. The whole of the plant is covered in stinging hairs except for the roots. The hairs have a silica cap on them, so cutting them will invariably blunt a knife or scissors. You are much better to pull or break the plant.

How to collect

Nettles have various uses beyond food and the whole plant is useful. If you are collecting for food, take only the topmost and youngest leaves. Collect in the late spring when the new growth has really only just begun. otherwise theycan become a little stringy

When you have collected your nettles, give them a good wash and allow them to drain. They will freeze well but otherwise they should be used straight away. A couple of hours after picking, the stings become impotent and you can handle them without worry. However, you can pat them between two towels to be doubly sure.

Medicinal uses

Nettles are really interesting plants when it comes to medicine. They are being used as a pain relief treatment for arthritis in some hospitals. Patients say they prefer the relief they get from arthritic pain over the stinging sensation. Also, although the stings contain histamine, the dried leaf is a good source of antihistamine, paradoxically providing relief from hayfever.

Tonic

The leaves are full of vitamins and are taken at a time when there is little else to be had, so they have kept people going through the hungry gap for millenia. It is interesting to note that many reports say the Romans

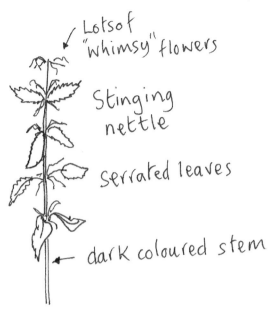

Lots of "whimsy" flowers

Stinging nettle

serrated leaves

dark coloured stem

brought the nettle to Britain. I'm not too sure about that and believe it to have been the case that nettles were first written about by them. Certainly the legions had the habit of bashing themselves on the legs with bunches of nettles to make them feel warm. What men! No wonder they defeated the known world!

Non-food use

We have already mentioned the rhizomes. They are stripped of their 'bark' and pulped with hammers to loosen the fibres and then soaked in a bucket of water. The paste is good for making paper. Alternatively they can he lightly bashed with a hammer and the fibres spun to make a very strong powerful rope.

The fibres in the stems can also be used to make cloth and the leaves, soaked in water, ooze a liquid that can be used as a hair tonic, a liquid fertiliser and a pesticide that is useful against aphids.

You can use nettles instead of spinach. Simply add the leaves to stews and pasta dishes. They will reduce down very easily.

Nettle soup

500g potatoes
1 large onion
250g young nettles
25g butter
75cl chicken or vegetable stock

Peel and chop the potatoes into 1cm cubes and wash and roughly chop the nettles. Slowly sweat the onions in the butter and, when translucent, add the nettles, stirring all the time. After a few minutes add the potatoes and the stock and bring to the boil. Simmer until the potatoes are cooked. You can blend or not, according to taste.

Nettle Tea

3 or four nettle leaves
3 or 4 dandelion leaves

Simply pour boiling water over the chopped leaves. This will be even better if you use an infuser. It is a great pick-me-up and, when you get used to it, is really refreshing.

Hair rinse

Nettle tea, made in larger quantities and without the dandelion, is a good rinse for dark hair. The mild, antibacterial action makes this an excellent anti-dandruff treatment.

Much veined leaf
dark green
with some yellow

5 petals all yellow

Primrose

Primrose
Primula vulgaris

The English primrose is such a wonderful plant that it gladdens the heart when it turns up in fields and by the roadside. This is one of the earliest flowers to appear in spring and can be seen almost throughout the year. It comes out so early that, at times, the flowers die before there are any insects about to pollinate it. Consequently, Shakespeare writes in a Winter's Tale of 'pale primroses that die unmarried.'

The leaves are large and acid green, lightly lobed and resemble cabbage leaves. They are crinkled between the veins and so look rather succulent. The flowers seem to be five lobed and joined at their bases. Various different forms of flowers appear, but they are all the same white/yellow colour.

You can use the leaves in salads but it is pot luck as to whether the flavour will be mild or bitter. The flowers make a lovely fragrant wine. Remember though, it is an offence to uproot this plant and if you do collect any flowers and leaves, do so sparingly. I do feel it is a shame, however, as the picking of primroses has been a part of our history, and reflects the way we interact with nature. Queen Victoria was said to have sent a box of primroses to Disraeli when he was dying. When asked if he would like the Queen to visit him he said, 'No, No! She'll only want me to give a message to Albert!'

Candied primrose flowers

Boil some sugar syrup, 500g sugar in aboiut 750ml water, and add the flowers. Using a fork, pull them out to dry. Keep the syrup. The following day put the flowers back for their second dunking in sugar syrup. Repeat this process at least three time. Store in a glass jar.

Rose hip
Rosa canina

Rosa canina is the dog rose but you can use any of the rosehips. These have long been used for food and wine making, as well as making rose water and candied sweets.

Although you wouldn't want to take advavtage of the fact, every bit of the rose is edible. Rose-hip wine and syrup is made from the fruit of the plant and is packed with vitamin C. Indeed, it is a most important source because there is more vitamin C in the rose than in any other plant. It is surpassed only by the common rat whose liver makes 1g of the vitamin every hour!

Roses are not difficult to recognise with their pink, five petalled flowers, intertwining in hedges with elder and hawthorn. Hedges are getting something of a bashing by modern control methods that are not kind to the plants therein. Anyone wishing to keep their length of

Rosehip
Orangehips
pink flowers

hedge as a larder should consider controlling it in the old fashioned way, with a mattock rather than a tractor and mechanical cutters.

The flowers appear in June and the fruits start to set by August, when they should be allowed to ripen for a month before taking them. They are lozenge shaped and about 2cm long.

You can collect rose-hips at any time from late summer through to autumn. Wear good gloves and make sure you only take the perfect hips.

Rosehip syrup

This is easy to make. You will need a kilo of rosehips, 500g sugar and a lot of water.

Collect the best rosehips you can find and clean off the stalks at the bottom and the black ends where the petals were joined to the ovary at the top. Chop into small 5mm pieces (you can use a food processor for this if you like) and add to 2 litres of boiling water. Boil for ten minutes and remove from the heat. Allow the hips to steep until cold. Drain the liquid through a muslin into a second pan and then boil the remaining pulp in an additional 1 litre of water for ten minutes. Cool and drain the liquid into the first batch.

Boil this down until you only have a litre left and then carefully add the sugar, stirring and boiling all the time.

Prepare some sterile bottles and pour and seal the syrup while boiling.

Beware sugar burns. When you cool a saturated solution of sugar from boiling, the crystals start to align themselves instead of being random. This gives out a lot of energy so, if you are splashed with sugar syrup, IT BURNS FOR A LONG TIME! Make sure you have cold water on hand to treat such burns.

Rose petal pour

This is a wonderful treat on ice cream. You need to use old-fashioned roses because the Hybrid Teas and Floribundas don't smell that good.

Collect about 50g of petals (about 200 petals) and cut out all the horrid bits if there are any. Boil up a syrup of 250g of sugar in 200ml water with the juice of a lemon, or an orange or two limes.

Then add the petals and boil for 15 minutes on a low light, stirring frequently so the bottom of the pan doesn't burn. You can add a knob of butter if you get a lot of froth. Pour into a sterile container and spoon onto ice cream. Then eat dressed in an Edwardian suit while sitting on a white cloth in the countryside after a tea of bread and butter, cakes and home made beer. Don't forget the boater!

Sloe
Large black/purple
berries
Watch the thorns!

Sloe (Blackthorn)

Prunus spinosa

The scientific name for this plant gives the name away. Blackthorn has the most murderous spines in the world which are fantastic at keeping people and stock away.

It is an ancient plant in the UK and, consequently, has a great deal of folklore associated with it. It is said that an angel transformed a base bush into the blackthorn to encourage Adam and Eve after their expulsion from Eden. It is true that the tiny flowers the blackthorn sends out at any time from February to April are very heartwarming. The spirit of blackthorn is supposed to cheer, especially those who are terminally fed up.

The thorns do have their uses, two of which I would like to talk about. Firstly they were used extensively as an awl to put holes in leather. They were also used to 'spike' horses. That is, placed under the saddle in such a way that, when the prospective rider sits on his mount, the thorn jabs the horse and sends it flying.

It is a member of the rose family and consequently each little white flower has five petals and it has between five and twenty little flowers all together. It is common in hedges and is more or less the first plant to flower in the late winter, early spring. The bark is very black and dark and the wood is heavy and hard. By June there are green fruits on the plants, which swell to about 1cm. They become ripe in late September, when they can be collected.

Sloes in honey are a wonderful tonic, which has been used for centuries as a winter pick-me-up. Simply collect around 50 berries and slice them, removing the central seed. You need to slice them into thin slithers. Then add these to a jar of honey – preferably local honey. A teaspoonful a day makes a sweet tasting, pleasant tonic that helps keep all sorts of maladies at bay.

The fruit is acidic, so much so that you could probably not eat it on its own. But it is made into a bewildering variety of jams, jellies and alcoholic drinks.

Sloe jelly

You will need about 3kg of sloes. Cut them in half, remove the stones and place in a preserving pan. Simmer with just enough water to not quite cover the fruit. Mash the fruit while you do this.

When the fruit has been mashed and boiled for about 30 minutes, strain completely through a double layer of muslin, getting all the flesh out. Measure all the liquid and weigh out an equal amount of sugar i.e., 500g sugar for 500ml liquid.

Bring to the boil and add the sugar. Check for a setting point as for jam and, when ready, pour into sterile bottles.

Sloe Gin

This is a wonderful and easy to make drink. Collect and wash your sloes and prick them all over with a fork. Weigh them and add to them an equal weight of sugar. Simply half fill a kilner jar (or several kilner jars) with dry sugar and dry sloes. Then fill the jar with gin. Actually you can also use vodka or brandy. Give them a shake up to help the sugar dissolve and leave them for as long as you can resist, the longer the better.

Sorrel
Rumex acetosa

Sorrel is one of those plants that people have depended on for a pot herb for a long time. The plant is tall growing and bears a lot of tiny flowers and seeds on the uppermost part. The leaves are long and look like the points of old fashioned lances, and are therefore described as lanciolate.

The plant contains a little oxalic acid, so people with arthritis and joint problems should avoid eating it raw. The oxalic acid gives the plant a lemon flavour and it has traditionally been used to put off feelings of thirst by farm workers.

The plant grows on the edges of fields, usually in disturbed soil. It can reach a height of around 60cm and is available right the way through the year, particularly if the winter is mild.

The stems of sorrel can be a little tough, but they very soon break down when cooked.

Sorrel and nettle stuffing

Purple brown
flowers in leaf axils

Sorrel

← Large lobed
pointed at end

Collect about 100g of each plant. Sweat off a very finely chopped onion in a little butter and finely chop the sorrel and nettle leaves. (wear gloves!) Season the frying onions and incorporate the shredded leaves into them, turning them frequently. Turn the heat down and don't let the leaves burn. Use this stuffing particularly for trout.

Sorrel sauce for fish

You have to enter into a strict training programme for this one. Melt 50g butter in a pan on a low heat and incorporate 100g shredded leaves. As the leaves cook, slowly incorporate 100ml double cream into the pan and beat rhythmically to mix well. Season and serve with either salmon or trout. You can add half a teaspoon of mustard powder for a little extra sharpness.

Sorrel soup

Roughly chop 500g sorrel and sweat in 50g butter with a finely chopped onion. Then slowly add 1 litre of chicken or vegetable stock and heat just below a simmer for twenty minutes. Season to taste. Then incorporate 50ml double cream and keep on the lowest heat for another 10 minutes.

Violet
Viola odorata

Everyone knows violets appear in the spring in little clumps that gladden the heart. The garden, woodland edge, even the field, are all good spots for these plants. The flowers are five petalled and usually violet in colour (of course) but you can also include the pansy, Viola tricolour, in this group. The flowers taste just as they smell, and are lovely candied. To do this you must take great care to be extremely delicate.

Candied Violet

Wash the flowers and remove the calyx and anything else green in colour. Spray with water and then roll in caster sugar. Repeat this process every day for a week and you should end up with a beautifully delicate little sweet. Brilliant for the top of cakes or just for eating.

The leaves are a bit thick but they do make a good addition to a salad, though they are a little tasteless. You can cut the leaves into fine strips and add them to a stew. They give off a thickening agent that will make the gravy more robust. For this reason you can add the leaves to jams that refuse to set.

Wild Garlic
Allium ursinum

You can smell this plant for miles and it is probably one of the best foods from the wild. When you think of wild food it conjures up pictures of people collecting and eating the food there and then, standing by a bramble as they pick away, eating a few and placing the remainder in a bag. Wild garlic, or Ransoms or Jack-by-the-hedge (although this last title is given to a few plants) is a required ingredient for many dishes, but you would need to be very hungry indeed to eat it raw.

Botany
Wild garlic is a member of the onion family, Alliums. Like all these groups they have a bulb and throw up a lily-like leaf from a central, wrap-around stem. On the top they bear white star shaped flowers which give off the familiar arom of garlic. However, all the rest of the plant smells strongly too.

It grows in damp soil close to running water. You should expect to find it on either side of a brook that flows into a river. It is nearly always found in clumps of a couple of hundred plants in woodland and grows very well in the shade.

Unlike commercially grown garlic, which has a large, well-developed bulb (botanically speaking – a collection of corms), wild garlic has a much less developed bulb and the whole plant tastes strongly of garlic.

Health
The substances that give it its garlic flavour are called

allicins. They are complex molecules based on sulphur. During the first quarter of the twentieth century these substances were the 'must have' drugs for fighting infection. Allicins are indeed antibiotic and antiviral and it was only the discovery of penicillin that brought research in garlic to an end.

Researchers truly believed they had found a miracle drug, but now doctors are returning to garlic in the fight against super bugs and resistant strains of bacteria. During the First World War bandages of garlic and wild garlic were used as field dressings which saved many lives.

Allicins have been found to reduce blood pressure, 'un-harden' hard arteries and improve health. Eating garlic is one of the important health strategies, and this is also true of wild garlic in particular.

Collecting
Only collect what you need. Find as many strands as you can of this plant so you will not cause too much damage to the local population. Remember that it is illegal to uproot this plant, but you can take some leaves – which should suffice. Wild garlic is chopped and all parts of the plant can be used.

Simply cut off a piece of leaf from various plants and put them in a sealed container. They will keep for a week or more in the fridge.

Use
Simply wash and chop the whole plant (or whatever part of the plant you have) and use instead of garlic. The leaves do not fry quite so well as onion or chopped garlic, and they need slightly less heat. They do impart

a garlic flavour to oil and other dishes in precisely the same familiar way.

You will need a leaf to replace a clove of standard garlic. However, you can also use the leaves to make garlic flavoured crispy bits. Simply cut the leaf lengthways and lightly fry it.

Wood Sorrel

Oxalis acetosella

At first glance you would be forgiven for mistaking this plant for clover. The leaves are trifoliate in the same way, but they are much bigger and hang down. They are also heart shaped rather than round or oval as in clover.

They bear pretty flowers too, although the leaves are slightly lemony and acidic to taste. They are high in oxalic acid, in fact more so than rhubarb leaves, but this is reduced by cooking. Oxalic acid stops you from digesting other nutrients, so you should only consider taking this plant if you are young, fit and healthy.

In small quantities these leaves make a really thirst quenching addition to a salad, and the flowers, which have a slightly bell like appearance with five petals, can also be added to salads to make them look pretty.

It is said that the leaves act as a febrifuge, which means that they are good at relieving a fever.

Chapter Three
New Leaves for Old

When we eat plants it is usually the leaves we consume and we tend to eat only a few types. Cabbage, lettuce, rocket and maybe a few others if we are particularly adventurous, like vine leaves. Of course we drink a few more in the form of tea and make soup from a few more still. But what follows are examples of leaves that can be found in nature that we can use in the kitchen.

Cabbage alternatives

The thing about cabbage is that it looks different, according to its environment. For instance, a cabbage grown in a confined pot will grow long and thin and will look much more like oilseed rape. Cabbages grown in a lot of space will grow like a ball, all tight and round.

There are a number of cabbage alternatives including nettle and, more importantly, rosebay willow herb.

Rosebay willowherb
Epilobium angustifolium

The plant is tall and bears a cone of flowers at the top. It has long (8cm), thin leaves at points all around a single stem. The young leaves are the best to take, and should be boiled and served up just like cabbage but do not drink the water because it can provoke an allergic rash in some people.

You can also use the young shoots as a very good alternative to asparagus.

Rosebay tea

To make this you have to dry the leaves. This is best done slowly on a window sill on a piece of kitchen roll. The leaves are then rubbed together to make a decent 'tea' which is frequently drunk in both Russia and Asia.

Plantain
Plantago ssp.

All the plantains are more or less edible. They can resemble a mixture between bistort and grass. The flower stalks bear lots of tight green flowers and the leaves that come from the base of the plant are either highly lobed, highly serrated or highly indented.

It is the leaves that are used as a vegetable. Simply collect them and wash and cook like cabbage, although they do need less cooking and can be bitter tasting.

Wild cabbage
Brassica oleracea

Wherever the Romans went they grew their version of cabbage, which spread into the wild quite easily. Today, wild cabbage matches almost exactly the distribution of the Romans in the UK – wherever they had a settlement, there you will find wild cabbage in the countryside, even today.
It is an evergreen perennial, about 1.2 metres tall. The leaves have a stronger flavour than the cultivated cabbages. Their flavour is somewhat sharper than ordinary cabbage, but they bear the same yellow flowers. If you do find a strand of wild cabbage, take

only a few leaves and at infrequent intervals. In this way the plant will regenerate and live for quite a few years. Pull off too many and you will lose it in a season.

You can use wild cabbage instead of ordinary cabbage, but it is probably best to do something special with it, if only because it is itself somewhat special. Why not try to use the leaf as a parcel in which you steam a piece of fish? It works particularly well with cod or any white sea fish, and is particularly good with eel and pike.

Campanula species.

Campanula are the bell flowers but NOT BLUEBELLS which are actually poisonous! The leaves are all edible, but this very large genus contains many very lovely ornamental plants and is very popular in gardens.

They are easy to grow and should be used far more widely than they are, but this knowledge of them is not that widespread these days

Harebell
Campanula persicifolia

This is a surprisingly large plant for one so delicate. The bell is borne on a very slender stem that trembles in the wind. They are very beautiful plants indeed and grow along the woodland edge, but can also be found in hedges and on moorland.
The leaves make for a great salad, and are even better in a salad sandwich. They have a mild sweetness to them that accompanies tomatoes a treat.

Musk Mallow
Malva moschata

Mallows are found growing by the woodland edge and in gardens all over the country. They grow to about 2 metres tall and have delicate flowers with a very distinctive set of crinkled petals. The anthers and stamens make a central feature that almost makes the flower look like a very pretty satellite dish.

The leaves are highly decorative with lots of lines and indentations in them. They can be used salads and have a mild flavour. However, they are really helpful for the digestive system and the kidneys and, in herbal medicine in particular, they are highly praised for their benefit to the liver.

You can eat as much of them as you like but the younger leaves are the best ones to eat. If you cut the stem, others will appear, bearing new leaves, so this plant will provide you with a summer's worth of food on a cut and come again basis.

The leaves are good right through to the end of October, when they start getting tatty and a little boring, not to mention eaten away.

Lime Tree
Tilia ssp.

We have already mentioned the Lime tree, otherwise known as the Linden tree. The young leaves make excellent lettuce alternatives. The suckers are most useful on this plant, and are without doubt the best way of collecting the leaves because you can more or less be sure that they are young leaves.

The plant is often infested with aphids, exuding their sugary honeydew so loved by bees and wasps. This makes the leaves unusable because the honeydew also attracts a fungus that can be poisonous or will at least spoil the leaf.

Miner's Lettuce
Montia perfoliata

This is a crazy looking plant that has leaves that wrap around the stem in discs, so it looks as though someone has strung a lot of varying sized coins on a green string. It bears tiny white flowers in the axils of the leaves. There is also a completely different set of leaves at the base of the plant that look a little like spears, or plantain leaves.

The leaves are bland but not unpleasant and at least as tasty as lettuce. Take the youngest ones as ever. As the summer continues the leaves will increase in bitterness. By the way, you can also use the root system and the bulbs that form, but they are a bit time consuming to prepare. These taste like chestnuts.

Chicory
Cichorium ssp

The leaves look like dandelion leaves gone mad, with all sorts of angles to them. The flowers are borne on the side of the stems and look like mauve daisies.

Lovers of Camp coffee will know this flavour well. It is also grown as a garden plant and is quite widespread in the wild.

It forms a rosette of leaves up to 50cm tall, though when flowering it sends up a shoot that can be 1.5 metres tall. Chicory leaves taste very bitter and are best when just blanched and dried and thrown into salads. They can also be sliced small and used almost as a salad condiment – just enough to make a green salad interesting, but not enough to make you gag.

Chicory leaves are very healthy, much more so than dandelion or lettuce, and should perhaps be included in all mixed salads.

Chapter Four
Fungi

There are so many fungi in the world that it is impossible to know them all. Fungi include some of the largest living things on the planet. One individual has been measured in square miles. Of course, this is the fungal hyphae, those microscopic filaments that ramificate through the soil and rotting material. To date, no one has found a five square mile mushroom!

Scientifically speaking, since they don't move like animals, fungi have been placed firmly in the plant kingdom. However modern science places them in a kingdom of their own, a far more proper way of looking at them. Mushrooms are important for a number of reasons. First of all they help break down dead material, releasing their nutrients into the soil. They also affect plants, helping them absorb nutrients that they otherwise would not be able to access. Many plants simply cannot grow successfully if the correct fungus is absent. The bluebell and many cabbages need appropriate fungal partners to thrive.

Collecting fungi

You need to be aware of the major killers. The Death Cap and the Destroying Angel are the two major causes of concern. Another way of looking at it is to collect only those mushrooms you are completely sure of recognising properly.

Do not store your bounty in plastic bags; the number

of cases of food poisoning resulting from rotting, but otherwise safe, fungi is much greater than those of straight poisoning from unsafe fungi. Collect only perfect specimens, and if you are not sure, leave them well alone!

Do not dig the mushroom out of the soil. This will only damage the mycelium, those tubules that make up the bulk of the organism. Also always give the mushroom a good tap as this allows any creepy crawlies and fungal spores to fall out.

Where to find fungi

Fungi grow anywhere. You are most likely to find them in woods where there are plenty of rotting trunks. Different types of woodland have their own unique fungi. If you have pine woodland that is sandy you will have an excellent foraging habitat. But you can also find mushrooms in other habitats such as grasslands, farmland and ground that has recently been burned.

The mushroom structure

When it is first formed the mushroom is covered in a membrane called the Universal Veil. This breaks off and you can see where it breaks off at the bottom of the stem because it leaves behind a cup of tissue attached to the base of the stalk.

The cap on the top of the mushroom, the umbrella if you like, is also attached to the stem until the cap expands and breaks free. This leaves a tissue all around the stem called the ring. The cap itself has a topside and an underside. The topside may or may not have scales on it and the underside might have gills or tiny holes rather like a pepper pot. Sometimes the holes are so small that the whole mass resembles a tiny sponge.

The combination of these structures will determine whether you should pick the mushroom.

The Destroying Angel and Death Cap mushrooms are deadly. The treatment of choice is a liver transplant within a day of being sick and even then it might not help! Be warned! Be very careful what you do with mushrooms.

Recognising the Death Cap
All parts of this fungus are deadly, and you shouldn't touch it.

The cap starts out yellowish and turns olive green or can become white with a green tinge. Underneath the cap it is lightly veined and snakeskin like in appearance, with a series of dark lines under the cap.

On the young mushroom the cap is very convex but flattens out later. The mushroom has a sweetish smell and may appear to be sticky. The gills underneath the cap are white, and the very white stem has a distinct ring, although one or two examples might just have no apparent obvious ring.

The base of the stem bulges into a bulb that is covered by a membrane rather like a sheath. Sometimes the green can look almost yellowish brown and sometimes the bulb may be under the soil. Sizes can vary immensely from just a little over a centimetre up to 8cm in diameter. Unless you are very certain of what you have found, take no risks. Speculation can be deadly.

Recognising the Destroying Angel
The mushroom is white. A white cap, stalk and gills.

In fact strikingly white. The cap might be yellowish, pinkish, or even tan towards the centre, but the outside is most definitely white.

When the mushroom is young it is covered by a universal veil and this makes it look like a small puffball. If you cut it in half the Destroying Angel has mushroom parts inside, waiting to grow out. The puffball, on the other hand, is simply a uniform cream coloured material with no distinct anatomy inside. Always cut what you think is a puffball to check this.

The gills under the cap are not attached to the stalk and the base of the stalk has the remnants of the universal veil. The cap is usually about 6–15 cm across. The stem is usually 8–20 cm long and about ½–2cm thick.

Join a group
There is no pleasanter a way of learning about mushrooms than alongside an expert. Around the UK there are a number of mycological or fungus societies. The County Wildlife Trusts also hold mushroom days around the country.

The Season
Any time of the year is good, though there is some seasonality for different types. Bracket fungi can be had from May to September, morels are available in river washed woodland from April to June, and from the winter into spring, agaric mushrooms are available.

Above all, perfect mushrooming weather is warm and wet. Long periods of drought do not produce much in the mushroom line.

Mushrooms to collect and eat

For the very beginner I shall describe a dozen different edible ones with which you cannot go wrong. Wherever you collect mushrooms and whatever they are, do not over gather them. The spores are an important part of the life cycle of the fungus and if you consistently collect all of them, then the fungus will slowly die.

Avoid if you can

To be completely safe I would avoid collecting small, whitish mushrooms, anything slightly greenish, or anything very white that looks like an ordinary mushroom you can buy. Avoid also the spotty red mushrooms until you can tell the difference between a blusher and a fly agaric. (No, you'll not find either in here. I simply don't want to encourage you into a visit to the local emergency liver transplant ward.)

Finally, don't go anywhere near an earth ball – that is anything that looks like a potato, but when cut through appears white with developing black spores. The Puff ball is much larger, (and yes, you will find the puff ball here!) Only take such mushrooms that are pure creamy white inside with no hint whatsoever of blackness.

Hopefully what follows will whet your appetite and convince you to become a field mushroom expert!

The Penny Bun or Cep

Boletus edulis

The Penny Bun has many names including the boring old 'Edible Boletus'. The French call it the cep, and this now sticks in the UK too.

Where to find it

This mushroom grows at the field edge of woodland. You will not really find it near cities, except in very rare cases, and it is to be found from July to October. You will find it a little way into the wood, along woodland streams and banks.

Description

There is a brown cap that looks as though it is a tiny cushion. It is between 5 and 15 cm across, but is likely to be closer to 5cm, larger ones usually being eaten by wildlife. The young mushroom is light brown and it slowly darkens as it dries. The skin of the cap also wrinkles as it browns. Underneath, the flesh that makes up the tubules is white on a new specimen, but turns a deep, creamy yellow with age. There are no gills underneath, just a series of fine tubules.

The stem looks like a little club, almost rounded at the bottom and narrowing slightly towards the cap. The flesh of the stem is white or grey, turning a light creamy brown. It is very tough. If you look closely you will find a light brown network, almost lace-like, under the surface.

You will hardly ever find a fully mature penny bun that has not been eaten by beetles and flies. But this shouldn't matter – simply cut away any offending parts.

Don't confuse

This mushroom looks like a few others, but the penny bun's flesh under the cap doesn't bruise when you hit it. Also, the flesh of the penny bun remains creamy white to creamy yellowish. Others turn either pinkish or purpleish.

Penny bun grill

This is such an easy thing to do. Take a penny bun and slice it in half. Wash and dry with kitchen roll. Then brush with olive oil and sprinkle with a little salt.

Place under a hot grill and toast each side for one minute.

Bay Boletus
Boletus badius (formerly Xerocomus badius)

This is sometimes incorrectly referred to as the cep in some books.

Where to find it
It is very common in woodland, particularly coniferous woods. They have been found in profusion under beech trees and spruces too. This mushroom can be found deep in the woods.

Description

It resembles all the other boletuses but is a nutty chestnut brown on the cap. The young ones even seem to be downy, as though they were made of velvet. It is about 5 – 12cm across. The cap continues to open out throughout its life, becoming almost like a parasol at maturity. There is frequently a little depression where the stalk holds the cap.

There are no gills, but many tubules which turn blue when you press them with the thumb.

The stem is about 2cm wide, up to 8 cm tall and varies in basic colour from creamy white to brown. There are not many veins inside and all the flesh is white inside, possibly with a tinge of blue.

Don't confuse

This is a hard one to confuse for a dangerous mushroom, save for a Tylophillus species, which has a pink edge to the cap and is more squat and robust looking. If your mushrooms taste bitter, then this little beggar has gotten into your bag, and you need to throw the lot.

Baked Bay Cap

Fry some breadcrumbs, garlic and finely chopped onion together until golden brown. Drizzle olive oil over the caps and stuff with the mixture. Add a little salt and pepper and place in a hot oven at 200ºC for 15 minutes. 2 each make a great starter.

Slippery Jack
Suillus luteus

This is also known as the ringed boletus because of its distinctive ring, formed when the cap left the stem. It is known as the slippery Jack because the cap is slimy, even in dry weather.

Where to find it
This fungus exists in a very strong symbiotic relationship with the Scotts pine (Pinus sylvestris) or the Northern pine (Pinus montanus), and you are most likely to find it growing at the base of these trees from July to September.

Description
The cap is light brown to chestnut colour and the slimy part of the cap is easily peeled back. There are no gills, and the tubules form a yellowish cream flesh. The pores are very regular in shape and are five or six sided. The stem is around 6cm and, at the top above the ring, there is evidence of tiny brown spots or speckling. The ring on the stem is very obvious and the flesh has a pleasant odour and is slightly sour in flavour.

Don't confuse
As long as you look for a mushroom that has no gills but pores, a definite ring and a very slimy cap, you can't go wrong.

Slippery Jack linguini

Four slippery Jacks per person(or mix with any other mushrooms to make 550g.

Melt 25g butter in a frying pan on a medium light and

add three crushed garlic cloves and half an onion, finely chopped. Cook for just 30 seconds. Slice the mushrooms into ribbons and add to the pan and cook for another 10 minutes. After which time you add 200ml double cream.

Have some linguini (or your favourite pasta) on the boil ready for serving and simply combine the two with a little cheese and seasoning.

Birch boletus
Leccinum scabrum

This is also known as the rough legged boletus. The stem is marked with tiny scales which can be light brown to almost black. It makes good eating when young but tends to get messy and spongy and falls apart during cooking when old.

Where to find it
This fungus lives in a symbiotic relationship with birch trees, in particular the silver birch, Betula alba. It is to be found in woodland and gardens around the base of the trees and is common from mid-summer to the onset of winter. Since dwarf birches grow on moorland, this mushroom is also common on moorland where it assumes a much lighter appearance.

Description
The cap is every shade of brown, from cream to chestnut, sometimes on the same mushroom. They are about 12cm in diameter and hemispherical at first, flattening out as they mature. The stem is distinguished by the scales – sometimes light but mostly dark in colour and all over the stem, making it look rough rather like old sandpaper.

The stems are quite long and thin in comparison to the cap – about 18cm in all.

Don't confuse
There is little problem here. All the mushrooms that have rough, scaly stems are edible, so don't worry. This goes for the red boletus, which is all but the same as the birch boletus but has a fiery orange-red cap.

Dried mushroom

Birch boletus is ideal for drying. You can do this in a number of ways. You can buy a desiccator that slowly dries the mushroom, you can put it behind glass in the garden or you can leave it in the oven at the lowest temperature you can get it to work on. Then the dried mushrooms can be wrapped in kitchen roll, placed in a plastic container and frozen.

Whenever you want a mushroom element to curries, soups and stews - just pull out a handful.

Hedgehog of the woods
Hydnum repandum

Where to find it
This is quite a common mushroom in all kinds of woodland from summer to autumn. You are most likely to find it in leaf litter on the woodland floor.

Description
It has neither gills nor pores, but the spores are borne on spines under the cap. It is the colour of bread, or creamy white. The caps are about 10cm across but they meld into other caps to create quite a large mass.

The spines under the cap are easily broken off and are about 5mm long. They are distinctly yellow.

The stalk is about 6cm long with a yellowish, creamy skin. The flesh inside is whiteish. It is best to choose younger specimens that are mostly grub free. The older they get, the more infestations they have which tends to make them unpleasant.

Don't confuse
There aren't many fungi with a similar description that would be considered dangerous.

Hedgehog roast

This is a simple roast of whatever vegetables you can get. Carrot cubes, whole garlic cloves, turnips, parsnips, some rosemary, potatoes etc. Simply fill a roasting tray and toss in the cleaned, cubed (about 1cm) vegetables, covering with whatever herbs you prefer.

Season with salt and pepper and sprinkle with olive oil. Bake in a moderate hot oven at 180 – 200°C for thirty minutes. Then turn the oven down to 150°C and

Many folded light brown /green

Lots and lots of tubes, no gills.

Wood Hedgehog — creamy stalk

liberally spread 250g of hedgehog mushrooms, chopped into reasonably small (about 1cm) pieces and cook for another 30 minutes.

Some recipes call for eggs to be broken over the surface after this stage, but I don't add them because there is only so much yumminess you can cope with in one lifetime!

Common Puffball
Lycoperdon perlatum

There are many puffballs with some larger ones weighing in at over a kilogram. The most important thing to remember is that if you slice through a puff ball type fungus it must remain completely white. The earth ball has blackness inside and is poisonous and another deadly fungus that, in its young days is covered with a universal veil, has mushroom parts inside and is in no way describable as uniform white flesh.

So the key point is make sure it is uniform tissue that is uniformly white.

Where to find it
The common puffball is found almost everywhere, particularly in wooded river valleys. They are also found on top of hills and in grassland – my first ever was actually in my own back garden.

Description
The common puffball is about 8 - 12cm high and resembles an upturned round bottomed flask as is used in so many school laboratories. The ball is around 8cm across and is covered with hundreds of little wart-like scales. The scales rub off easily and make a proper

mess of the bottom of the bag.

Don't confuse

So long as it is white all the way through and not black and shows no distinct anatomy inside, eat it. All the species that show this characteristic are edible.

The big problem are the wrigglies; thousands of insects and grubs of various sorts that are themselves eating their way through the mushroom too.

Puffball omelete

There isn't a lot of flavour in a puffball, but it collects flavours from elsewhere, so it makes for a great mixed omelette. Simply collect 50g of any of your favourite mushrooms and thinly slice them. Cut a slice out of your puffball and shred into strips, say 100g. In all you need about 300g of mushrooms for the whole omelette.

Beat six eggs (this serves three people) and get as much air into them as you can. Then slowly fry a small onion and some garlic in butter and after three minutes add the mushrooms, turning regularly. When they have changed colour and texture, add the egg, making sure that the whole of the pan is covered.

When the bottom of the egg is set, transfer it to the grill and cook the top. If you have put enough air into the beaten egg it should rise like a soufflé. A final sprinkling of 50g of cheese, finely grated, should melt beautifully into the foaming eggs to finish the dish perfectly.

Morel — the recticulations
look like folded sheets.

Morel
Morchella esculenta

To my mind there are few mushrooms to beat this
unusual and strange looking fungus.

Where to find it
You are most likely to find morels in woodland, either
coniferous or otherwise, where the land is sandy and
there is a decent amount of lime about. You can also
find them where there has been a fire. They appear in
late spring, particularly after rain.

Description
The cap is not dissimilar to the stalk in shape, often
tapering to a blunt point and is either golden brown
or dark grey (Morchella elata). The most striking
characteristic of the cap is that it is cris-crossed with
deep grooves and walls that give it the appearance of
a rough honeycomb. For this characteristic alone it
cannot easily be mistaken.

Don't confuse
One other mushroom does look a little like the morel, but it only grows in sandy conifer woods and hates lime. The cap is dark brown and actually looks like a brain, not a honeycomb.

Again, morels are full of wrigglies. These are best removed by soaking them overnight in salty water and then leaving them to dry.

Morels in butter

Put the diet away. Take 100g per person of morels and cut them in as many ways as you like. Heat up 50g butter and fry the morels on a low light. Turn the mushrooms frequently and season. Finally, stir in 50ml (or so – go on, be generous!) of double cream. Pull out the mushrooms and serve with a little of the sauce. You will need nothing else, save plenty of black pepper.

Chanterelle
Cantarellus cibarius

Where to find it
This is widely available throughout the country in all kinds of woodland, but sometimes turns up in fields and on road verges. It is in season from June to the onset of winter.

Description
From a distance this looks like someone has been throwing eggs. The cap is yolk yellow and is very folded and up to 12cm across. Under the cap there are no gills, but a series of ridges that look like veins. The underside resembles the flesh of some great monster that has been dipped in acid, revealing the veins. The

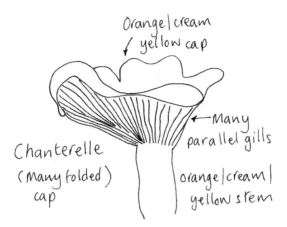

Orange|cream / yellow cap

←Many parallel gills

Chanterelle (Many folded) cap

orange|cream| yellow stem

stem is uniform in width, creamy yellow to creamy apricot-orange in colour and branches out into the cap.

Don't confuse

The false chanterelle looks a bit like it but, since it is not poisonous, I wouldn't worry about it. However, the false chanterelle is completely useless to eat, so the only thing you risk is a little disappointment.

Chanterelle red cabbage

What an accompaniment for duck this is! 500g shredded red cabbage is boiled for 5 minutes. Peel and fry 200g shallots cut in halves in 50g butter with a large tablespoon of sunflower oil. Drain and transfer the red cabbage to the frying shallots as they are just beginning to caramelise. Chop 200g of chanterelles into 2cm pieces and add this to the cooking cabbage. Stir frequently. After a few minutes add a good handful of raisins and cook for another three minutes.

Horse mushroom

Agaricus arvensis

This is a big beggar! You will be struck by its size more than anything else.

Where to find it

This fungus is very widespread, and you will find it at the edge of woodland, in fields and under plants in the garden. The cap is 25cm across and bell shaped at first, but slightly convex later. It is white and then turns yellowish. The main thing about this mushroom is that when you cut it it turns yellow at the wound. There is also usually a very distinct ring and the gills start grey white, turning pinkish red and then chocolate brown. The stem is up to 15cm long.

Don't confuse

This can look a little like the destroying angel, but the yellow flesh test should be enough to determine this, and the cap is also much bigger. If in any doubt at all, please pass it by. Who wants a liver transplant or a painful death as the price for a plate of mushrooms?

Cooking with horse mushroom is a little boring. There are no great reasons to use it in any other way than ordinary mushrooms.

The Parasol

Macrolepita procera

It looks like a gnome's umbrella. What more can you say?

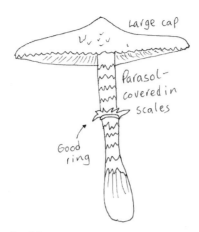

Where to find it
It is often at the edge of woodland and in clearings, especially where fire has disturbed the ground.

Description
The cap is scaly and warty and is 30cm across. It has a distinctive bump in the centre of the cap, which looks like the top of a parasol. However, this can flatten out. It sometimes resembles a great jellyfish, too. When young it looks like a ball on the end of the long stalk.

The stem is slender and about 30cm long. It is rough skinned and looks a bit like bark on a tree. The flesh of the stem is tough and unpalatable. The gills are whiteish and not attached. It gives off a pleasant smell.

Golden fried parasol

Take one parasol per person. Beat 2 eggs per mushroom and have 300g of seasoned breadcrumbs available.

Wash the mushroom and dry. Dip in the beaten egg and dip immediately into the breadcrumbs. Fry in butter for 3 minutes each side and gobble up!

Blewit

Clitocybe nuda

Blewits do not look edible due to their colour. They are anything from lilac to purple, and from the start you begin to think of trouble. They have a short stem to which the gills are attached. Like many mushrooms of this type, the cap is convex when young and flattens out as it ages. The name means 'blue hat.'

Some books have said that blewits smells of oranges. They do have an odour and the nearest I can describe it is of orange lollies, but it is such a long time since I had one (the lolly that is) that I can hardly remember.

Don't confuse

It is possible, although the blewit is nearly the only mushroom you can see of that colour in the woods, that you might confuse it with a cortinarius. Though this isn't very likely. To be completely sure, tap the mushroom on some paper to release the spores. Blewit spores are whiteish, whereas the other's are a rusty brown. That and the smell will prove the point.

Cooking with blewits is simplicity itself. Simply fry them lightly in butter, season and then add a few tablespoons of cream to finish. Who needs a waistline anyway?

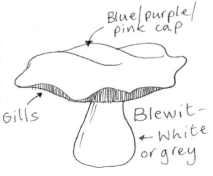

Blue/purple/ pink cap

Gills

Blewit - white or grey

Chapter Five
The Forager Goes Forth

1. Woodland

There are plenty of woodland walks that can provide us with all kinds of food. The word fodder, often used to describe animal food, comes from the word forage. The woodland is a perfect place to find food. Much of the food sources in the woods are dealt with elsewhere in this little book, and we need to bear in mind that, in a way, most things are edible in one form or another, even though now and again we come across something that is poisonous.

I would like to relate some woodland rules that you might find both interesting and useful as you enjoy our woodlands.

What to eat

Make sure that, on first eating something new, you only take a small amount no bigger than a penny in size. If this doesn't make you ill, try a bigger piece next time, which will have given you a chance to take a little home to find out all about it. Also, keep some of it with you, just in case you get into trouble. Do not make a meal of something you know nothing about.

Where to walk
In woodland you will find many paths. Stick to these. They are not always human paths, but could have

been worn down by foxes, badgers, rabbits and other residents such as deer. The paths provide a route that is fairly quiet, and this is the key. You will enjoy your walk through the woods much more if you too are quiet. Birds will fly past at head height and mammals will feed away, oblivious of your footfall. As soon as you tread on a stick the piercing crack will meander through the trees to warn everything around that there is a great fat clumsy human blasting his way through the scene. This being the case, you will think there is nothing but trees in the wood at all.

Water

On the whole the water in a wood, unless it is fast flowing and mountainous, is not worth drinking. Leaf litter makes it brown and acidic and it can be quite rancid. It is much better to take your water from fruits growing on the trees.

Flowers and plants

Herbaceous plants in woodlands tend to have a hard time of it, being fair game for rabbits, deer and almost every other herbivore. The sparse ground vegetation tends to protect itself largely by being poisonous but of course there are exceptions; we have already mentioned wild garlic. But plants like bluebells, no matter how succulent the bulbs may seem, are very poisonous indeed.

Beech

Fagus sylvatica

The beech is a huge tree that will grow to as much as 40 metres in height and will take over 120 years to reach it. Interestingly, the beech produces nuts in a cycle of five to eight years and some years there are more than others. The bark is smooth and light grey in colour and you can see up into to the canopy. The nuts, which are available from September onwards, are wrapped in a thick, spiked cover called a cup. They fall to the ground in profusion.

Also the young leaves, those that come in March and April, are edible too; simply use them in salads.

The nuts are full of oil, which can be got at by grinding and then pressing them. The oil is excellent for cooking.

The nuts are eaten raw, and are very sweet. They can also be cooked by baking them in the oven or roasting over a fire. Beech nuts should not be consumed in a gluttonous way. There are reports on the internet that people who have eaten 50 or more have fallen ill.

Beech nut bake

Fry a large, finely chopped onion in three tablespoons of olive oil. After a couple of minutes add a few chopped garlic cloves.

This is an easy vegetarian roast that anyone can enjoy. It contains a handful of each of the following: beech nuts, walnuts, pecan nuts, peanuts, raisins, chopped mushrooms.
Break up the nuts. I find the best way of doing this is to put them is a bag and bash them with a rolling pin.

Add all the ingredients to the frying onions when the onions are translucent. Combine everything and then transfer the whole lot to a large flat tureen. It needs to be around 2cm deep. ,

Transfer to the oven and bake for 30 minutes at 180°C.

Birch
Betula ssp.

The birch is probably one of the commonest trees in the country, from the white bark of the silver birch to the darker bark of the larger ones. The plant has edible leaves when they are young, but you wouldn't want to eat them. Those of you who make your own skins will be able to use the bark in the tanning process. The real reason for including the tree in this book, though, is the sap. Birch sap wine is really good stuff.

Birch sap wine

Simply drill a hole 2-4cm deep into the plant in spring and insert a plastic hose. The hole needs to be at a 45 degree angle going upwards into the tree. Really keen alcoholics might consider buying a birch sap tap! The sap can be collected into a demijohn or a bucket and, when it is full, plug the hole.

If you have a demijohn of sap, add 500g sugar and the juice of a lemon. Some recipes call for apple juice which you can add at a ratio of 1:1.

Bring the mush to the boil in a pan and then cool before pouring into a fermentation vessel with some yeast. Ferment and rack in your normal way.

Bugle

Wild
Garlic

Horseradish

Primrose

Chanterelle

Parasol

Morel

Penny Bun

Common Puffball

White Clover

Cuckoo Pint

Heath

chamomile

Burdock

Hawthorn

Medlar

Bluel

Rowan

Yew

Reedmace

Wood Sorrel

Mahonia

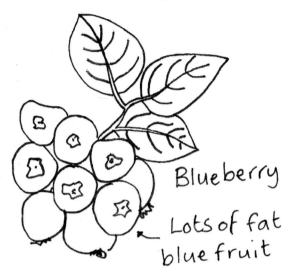

Blueberry

Lots of fat blue fruit

Blueberry
Vaccinium ssp.

Blueberries are woodland plants that grow up to 1.5 metres tall. They have small, dark green leaves borne on a woody series of stems. The leaves look a little like privet leavesbut are perhaps a mite smaller. When they are ready to harvest, from late August onwards, they are covered in masses of dark blue fruit about the same size as a raisin.

They tend to prefer acidic soils, and this makes them ideal candidates for food plants where there are a lot of rhododendrons in the woodland. They also grow well where the soil is boggy. They tolerate shade really well, but can also be found on the woodland edge.

The fruit is at its best when cooked with an equal weight of sugar and then used in a crumble. They also mix well with apples.

Elder

The Elder is a magical tree, so magical in fact that the fairies are said to make their musical instruments from the branches. If you fall asleep under its branches you will be transported to fairyland, so watch out. Being white flowered, the tree is said to protect all who live near it, especially if it had seeded itself. The pithy centres of the branches are easily bored out to make whistles and things for us mere mortals. For this reason the tree is known as the pipe tree or the bore tree.

It has had many names over the ages, *hylder* from Anglo Saxon, the *ellhorn* or *hldrum* of Saxony and its scientific name is *Sambucus nigra*.

The water that splashes off the leaves is also said to be magical, particularly for ladies of a certain age. It is said to revive beauty and I'm all for that! Simply wash your face in water collected from the plant in a rainstorm; it is supposed to work wonders.

The aroma of elder is very effective at deterring insects, and so sprigs of leaves used to be hung in doorways, barns and windows. They were also attached to bridles to help horses on hot days. However, the flowers are pollinated by flies and have an aroma designed to attract them.

Botany
Elder is a member of the honeysuckle family, though the flowers are quite different. It is a quick growing, low-branched woody shrub really, growing to around 4 metres in height. The flowers are set together in umbels – that is a group of flowers that are bunched together in an umbrella shape. The individual flowers

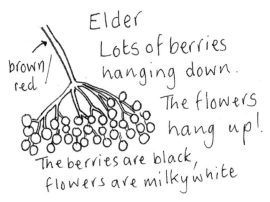

Elder
Lots of berries
hanging down.
The flowers
hang up!
brown/red
The berries are black,
flowers are milky white

are around 5mm across and the whole umbel is around 10 to 20cm across. It grows in hedges, coppices and woods, and is particularly happy growing around or near water – canal banks are a favourite habitat.

The bark starts out grey and becomes brownish as it ages, ending up quite brown. The leaves are very complex with two or three opposite leaflets on either side of a central stalk and a singlet at the end making up the whole leaf. So each 'leaf' is made from five or seven leaflets. The individual leaflets are long and oval, but pointed at the end. Each leaf is highly toothed at the edges.

How to collect
The Elder is collected at the flowering stage and the fruiting stage. Elderberries make a good, rich wine and a fantastic cordial. They are probably one of the richest plants in vitamin C there is. The berries are dark red, almost black, and you should collect them only when they are full, undamaged and almost black.

The fruits, like the flowers, are borne on a series of stalks. Simply cut off the main umbel and put the fruit carefully into a bucket.

Collecting the flowers calls for a little judgement. Only pull off the milky white plants. Once the flowers are pollinated they turn a darker cream colour, look less appetising and smell more strongly. Pull the whole of the umbel off the branch.

Remember, if you take all the flowers on the plant there will be no berries later in the year, so leave a few. Also, leave some for the birds to eat.

If you are making elderflower wine, simply use the whole umbels and don't try to take the individual florets off the plant. You can remove the berries from the umbels using a fork. They break down easily and stain the fingers.

Medicinal uses

The berries are high in vitamins A and C are so lovely that the cordial can be used to mask any other medicines.

Hay fever
The flowers, boiled in water to make a juice and served with a tablespoon of honey, will both soothe and inoculate against some of the pollen grains that cause hayfever.

Tonic
The high vitamin content, sweetened with honey and served warm, is not only soothing to take but is a general boost to the immune system, particularly for people who are recovering from illness, are old or just off colour and it is completely safe to take.

The plant is rather high in tannins and has to be processed in some way before consumption. The flowers and fruit are usually doused in boiling water before being made into drinks. The fruit is also cooked in pies. Do not try to eat more than one or two of the raw berries; apart from their being very sour you will also end up with a blistering bellyache.

Do not attempt to eat the leaves at all and do not feed them to your livestock. The fairies will definitely come in the night if you do!

Non-food use
The wood of elder has traditionally been so highly respected that it has not been used for anything except ornaments of a quasi-religious nature. The wood doesn't burn that well, and you are supposed to ask the fairy folk's permission if you try.

The dark coloured berries have long been used as a dye, but it is not very colour safe. If you decide to dye clothes with it you must use a mordant such as alum and in a good quantity too. Otherwise, any old acid speeds its oxidation to blues and purples. Sunlight also changes the colour of clothes dyed with elderberry.

Fencing and hedging
Elder is a major part of traditional hedges in the UK. They provide a sturdy anchor for other plants in the hedge and also open up the hedge for wildlife. They are often found on the corners of hedges and near gateposts.

Elderflower fritters

First you need to make a batter for the elderflower heads.
This is a fairly thin batter and should sit for a while.

Baking powder batter
150gm flour (of any type)
15gm Baking powder
Water to mix

Sift the flour and baking powder together, then add water
to make a fine paste. Add the water gradually so that the
batter doesn't become lumpy. Use a whisk to mix.

You can make yeast batter easily and this is more
traditional.

Yeast batter
150gm plain flour
10gm yeast
A teaspoon of sugar in a ¼ cup of lukewarm water

Add the yeast to the sugar water and leave to froth up.

Make a well in the flour and add the yeast mixture to
the well. Leave for 15 minutes and allow to grow. Add
around 150ml of water to the mixture and leave it to
settle for 30 minutes.

Either of these will make an excellent batter for the
flower heads. Simply dip the bright, fresh flowers into
the batter and then drain off the excess. From there
place them straight into hot fat.

They are great with sifted caster sugar.

Elderflower rosehip tea

One elderflower umbel
1 crushed rosehip
1 dessert spoon of honey

Normally rosehips are not on the plant at the same time as elderflowers but it really is worth collecting them because they are nature's highest concentration of Vitamin C. They will freeze quite easily and to make this tea all you need to do is defrost one and hit it with a spoon or a pestle a few times to crack it open a little.

Simply put a piece of elderflower umbel into a teapot with the rosehip and pour on boiling water. Then add the honey to your cup and stir in the tea. If you need some other flavour, a slice of lemon will suffice.

If you don't have rosehips, replace with a dessert spoon of rosehip syrup, still available form chemists.

Elderflower champagne
(knock your socks off wine)

4 large elderflower florets
200ml white wine base
1kg ordinary white sugar
5g citric acid
1 cup of strong tea
Wine yeast

Using a fork, strip the flowers off the stalks into a sterile bucket. Pour over 5 litres of boiling water and stir regularly for 24 hours. Dissolve the sugar into 500ml boiling water to make a sugar syrup. Strain the cool liquid into a second bucket through a muslin and add the sugar syrup.

Transfer the liquid to a demijohn and add all the other ingredients, giving the vessel a good shake to mix. If the demijohn needs to be topped up, use cool boiled water. Close the vessel with an airlock and stand on a tray in case the wine spills out when the fermentation starts.

When the bubbling has fully stopped, siphon off the liquid into a clean, sterilised demijohn, leaving the gunge behind in the bottom of the vessel. Top up with apple juice or boiled water. Close the new vessel off with an airlock and leave it for about six months (if you can bear to) and then rack off into bottles.

Keep your socks on wine

Not really alcoholic at all, but simply relying on natural yeast which survives immersion in the boiling water to ferment some of the sugar - you don't even need a demijohn for this one.

6 Elderflower heads
Juice and peel of 2 lemons
4 litres of boiling water
750g sugar

Put the elderflower heads and lemon peel into a bucket and pour on the boiling water. Leave to soak for 24 hours covered with a tea towel. Strain through a muslin and add the sugar and lemon juice. Stir until the sugar is completely dissolved and pour into two 2 litre screw-top lemonade bottles. Leave the tops slightly loose for a couple of weeks. Keep for 2 to 3 months before drinking. Serve cool on a hot summer evening.

Elderberry jelly

1kg elderberries
1 litre water
450g baking apples
Juice of one lemon
Sugar (1kilo for every litre of juice after straining)

Wash elderberries and remove stalks. Cut up the apples into small cubes. Don't bother to peel or core either. Put fruit and lemon juice in to a pan with the water and simmer gently for about an hour until soft.

Pour this into a jelly bag and leave to strain overnight.

Measure the strained juice and then add the appropriate amount of sugar. Stir until thoroughly dissolved and then boil for about 15 minutes.

Test for setting point by placing a teaspoon of the juice on a cold plate, cool a little and then push. If it wrinkles distinctly then it is ready.

You can then store in sterile jars.

Elderberry wine

2kg elderberries
5 litres boiling water
1.5kg granulated sugar
A sachet of brewer's yeast
Juice of 1 lemon
1 cup of tea (no milk)

Using a fork pull the berries from the umbel into a very clean bucket. Add the juice of a lemon and a cup of tea and cover with the boiling water.

Get in with your hands and squeeze all the juice out of the fruit. A potato masher will do just as well, but is less fun. Leave for one day to infuse.

Strain the liquid through a muslin cloth into another bucket (or a large pan) and then add the sugar, stirring all the time to make sure it is all dissolved. Strain into a demijohn and add the yeast. Stop with an air lock. When it has stopped bubbling, rack off into another demijohn and repeat this in a month to remove the lees.

I tend to serve this wine from the demijohn, but you can bottle it. Remember the wine is sensitive to light and should be bottled in green glass. It improves in the bottle if left for six months.

Hawthorn
Crataegus ssp.

There are many hawthorn species and each of them is a valuable food source because their fruit is an excellent food. It is also a wonderful source of pectin and is therefore an great starting point for jam and jelly making.

The plant is to be found all over the country in hedges and, where it is not managed, forms a tree up to 10 metres high. It is used in herbal medicine as a source of flavanoids and is put to use on ailments as diverse as heart disease, general health and complexion.

A number of clinical trials have taken place for people who take hawthorn to help with heart problems. The results have been mixed, but the largest, with a cohort of over 1000 people, did find that taking the extract provided some benefit. However, readers would be wise not to rely solely on this or to treat themselves.

Hawthorn makes a rather untidy bush and, in early spring, is covered in tiny white, five petalled flowers. The branches are smooth barked, dark and bear a lot of thorns – not so deadly as the blackthorn or sloe, but still making for an inpenetrable hedge. The leaves are lobed and sometimes serrated too.

The fruits are around 2–4cm across and look like miniature apples. They have different flavours according to the species used, but the British ones are a little sharp. Around the world the fruits are known as haws, but in the UK we hardly call them anything because we have forgotten their use.

The young leaves can be used in a salad if collected in April or May but do become tough and unpalatable from June onwards.

The fruits, which can be collected from late September, are yellow, orange or red in colour. You can eat them raw, but they are much better cooked, or used in jams and jellies.

Haw jelly

Fill a stockpot with haws and cover with water. Simmer until the fruits are quite soft. Pour the liquid through a jelly bag into another pot and for every litre of juice, stir in 500g sugar. Add a good knob of butter and, if there is any foam left, scrape it away.

Continue to cook the syrup until you get a setting point on a cold plate and then store in sterile jars.

Hazel
Corylus ssp

The Hazel is one of the most elegant trees in the wood. You can recognise it by the distinct, almost circular leaves. Little red catkins appear in February, long before the leaves in March and April.

The plant is traditionally a coppice tree. It is cut to its base so that lots of branches will grow. These branches grow straight and strong and do not rot when thrust into the ground. Hazel poles have long been used as an agricultural aid.

The hazel nut is a bit like a large peanut but with a dark skin. The flesh is very sweet, nutty and highly prized by squirrels. The nuts ripen into October when they can be taken.

Hazelnut praline

This is a simple process. Weigh your nuts and, for every kilo, use 500g sugar. Simply place the sugar and hazlenuts into a pan on a very low light, allowing the sugar to caramelise. Coat the nuts with the sugar and then pour into a greaseproof, paper lined tray and allow to set.

Alternatively, for a spooning product, bash the nuts into tiny pieces and add half their weight of honey, stirring all the time until they are completely mixed.

Juniper
Juniperus communis

Juniper is a conifer that grows to about 6 metres and produces lots of aromatic resin. It loves chalk, which mainly restricts its range to southern England, but can also be found in Derbyshire and parts of Yorkshire. It produces strange cones that look like berries which have a whitish bloom on them.

The bark is brown and crinkled and the 'berries' are around 1cm, bluish and fully round. They are available in September and October. The leaves look rather like a Christmas tree.

The wood and leaves are wonderful for smoking food, particularly fish. The berries are used to make gin.

Juniper is a mild diuretic and is also supposed to bring on contractions. 'Mother's ruin,' a vain attempt to induce abortion by drinking gin, never ever worked but is based on the fact that juniper berries can induce contractions. Breastfeeding mums should not take them, nor should children under 12 years because of their diuretic properties.

The berries can be used when cooking fish.

Juniper Salmon

Simply collect together equal quantities of juniper berries and black peppercorns and bash them in a pestle and mortar. The resulting mixture is rubbed into a salmon steak on both the flesh side and the skin side before simply frying in a minimum of oil.

Lime
Tillia ssp.

It was quite a long time before I realised that these plants didn't bear limes at all! They are trees that grow up to 6 metres high and bear fantastic flowers out of the leaves in a really interesting and unusual manner. The leaves themselves look just like the 'spade' sign on a pack of playing cards and are easy to recognise.

In the late spring, when the sap is rising, you can drill into the tree until the sap comes out. This is rich in sugar and, if you force a plastic pipe into the hole, you will fill a demijohn in a day or so. In times past this has been used to make sugar.

The leaves are edible and people used to collect them in order to make lime beer, which is so nasty (well mine has always been nasty) that I don't feel myself qualified enough to share it with you.

Most common limes are actually a cross between two species. Unusually they also send up suckers from the roots. These are really useful for making sticks of all kinds.

Mahonia
Mahonia aquifolium

Mahonia is now quite a common garden plant. It looks like holly and bears yellow flowers in clusters which are very sweet smelling. It differs from holly in that the leaves are born on stems that are much wider spread.

The flowers appear in the winter and it produces fruit

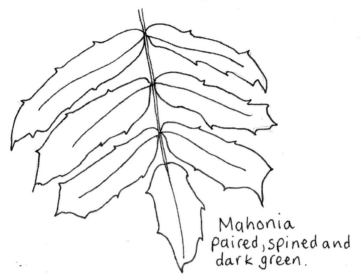

Mahonia
paired, spined and
dark green.

from summer onwards. These fruits are edible either raw or cooked and they are really delicious.

The fruits have a lot of seeds in them and they are slightly tart. It is the seeds that put people off, but you can make them into wine.

Mahonia Wine

Collect about 1kg of fruit and steep in sufficient boiling water to cover them. Bash the fruit with a masher and allow it to cool. Then strain through a couple of layers of muslin.

Top this liquid up to a gallon with apple juice and bring to the boil. Add 500g of sugar and, when cool, pour into a fermentation vessel. Add your yeast and allow it to brew out. Rack in the normal way and keep the wine for as long as you can! It is really refreshing!

Medlar
Mespilus germanica

This ancient plant was probably brought to the UK during the crusades. The tree grows up to 5 metres high and has long, boat shaped leaves. In late spring its five petalled white flowers resemble large, white, unkempt buttercups. The fruits are actually rather ugly, look like large, rotten rosehips and are borne on the tree from late August. They are also very acidic until later in the year when the first frosts or storage have ripened and sweetened them through enzyme action. Although they may look like some kind of deformed, almost rotten pepper pot, it is at this pointthat they are absolutely perfect! The idea that this fruit was rotten before its time made it a by-word for a prostitute.

You can tell this plant is not a rosehip by its leaves. If you see a bush that bears what looks like rosehips but has leaves rather like a less robust laurel, then you most certainly have a medlar.

Medlar jelly

Blett your medlars! Cut them open and you should see brown, mushy flesh. Cut all the fruit in half and fill a stock pot with them. Cover with water and boil for an hour. Then pour the juice into another pot through a double muslin. Then, for every litre of juice, add 500g sugar and bring to the boil. Test the juice for a setting point and then store in sterile jars.

Medlar port

Make the juice as described for the jelly and then add an equal amount of elderberry juice which has had sugar added to the same dilution. The juice of a lemon and a tablespoonful of yeast in a large fermentation vessel will set the brew going. Rack and re-rack in your usual manner.

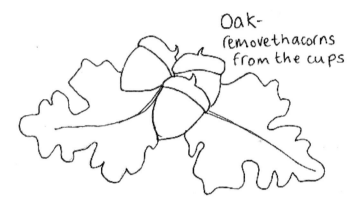

Oak-
remove the acorns
from the cups

Oak
Quercus robur

Everyone knows that great oaks come from tiny acorns; or is it the other way round? The oak is one of the UK's national emblems and everyone should learn to recognise its wavy leaf and acorn. The tree grows expansively over a wide area, sending out great branches that are frequently too heavy for the plant to bear. Oaks live to great ages and some of our oldest actually predate the British kingdom.

The plant is very heavy in tannins and these compounds, found in tea, can make you rather ill. Acorns are particularly full, and should not be simply taken and eaten. However, during times of hardship, people have taken acorns and used them for all kinds of food. They are ready for taking in October.

Acorn bread

I am not going to tell you how to bake with acorns, more rather how to make flour. Collect as many acorns as you can and remove them from their cups. Put them into a sack and bash them until they have broken up. Then place them into a bucket and fill with water. Allow the acorns to stand overnight and then drain the water. Repeat this process three more times (so they have been soaking in fresh water for four days) and then spread them out on a tray, a table, or on a cloth to dry.

Once they are dry you can then grind the acorns to make flour. This has been a substitute for wheat flour for many centuries.

Rowan

Sorbus aucuparia

The rowan is a majestic tree, not too large and bearing long leaves set like old fashioned palm branchlets. Each individual leaf looks like a fish-knife blade and the tree itself has a pleasant, upright stance. In the spring it is covered with thousands of milky white flowers that give way to orange fruit in the late autumn. The birds love them, particularly blackbirds. Back in the time when people ate blackbirds, the rowan's other name was the bird catcher.

The official name for the rowan is the mountain ash and it is to be seen in rock ledges and mountainous country just as frequently as in urban gardens and parks.

This is supposed to be a magical plant, bringing luck to every household. It was traditionally used as a back

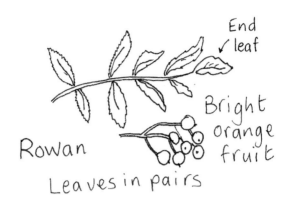

End leaf ✓

Bright orange fruit

Rowan

Leaves in pairs

door protector – not from thieves but elves! On May Eve rowan crosses were worn and placed on barns and doors to protect the inhabitants. The ancient age of this legend becomes clear as you learn that, to work correctly, the wood must be cut with stone. Rowan branches were brought indoors on Good Friday just like Christmas trees for protection against the spirits.

The fruit, when deep red, is an excellent source of pectin and rowan jelly was a favourite preserve in the Victorian kitchen, particularly since it can be used to set off other jams too.

Rowan jelly

Use equal quantities (about 1kg each) of rowan berries and good baking apples. Peel and core the apples and put the lot in a pot, cover with water and set to boil. Use a masher to break down the berries and boil for a good hour. Strain through a jelly bag into a second pan and, for every litre of juice, add 500g sugar. Bring to the boil and add a large knob of butter. Remove any froth and cook until you get a setting point on a cold plate.

Pour into sterile jars.

Sweet Chestnut
Castanea sativa

This large tree was originally a native of the Mediterranean region and was spread around Europe mostly by the Romans who liked it for its food. Certainly it was they who brought it to Britain. The tree grows up to 35 metres tall and the trunks can be 2 metres in diameter. There are some records of this plant living to great ages, the Tortworth Sweet Chestnut being 800 years old and with a girth of 11 metres.

Sweet chestnut wood is durable and can be used indoors and outdoors without treating, mostly on account of its density and high lignin content. The wood is traditionally used to make barrels.

The leaves are long and narrow and come to a definite point. Their edges are serrated and the whole leaf can be up to 20cm long.

The tree bears catkins of both male and female flowers and the nuts are housed in a casing covered in spines. The fruits can be collected from the ground by November. From a seed germinating in the ground it can be up to ten years before a new tree bears fruit, and for this reason our stock of chestnuts needs to be preserved.

Collecting
The nuts need to be prised from their casings and you will need gloves for this. You can then split the husks underfoot. Don't gather all the nuts from the floor or the tree; take only the best ones. Gleaning from nature means leaving some for other people, animals and the future too. You split the husks open underfoot.

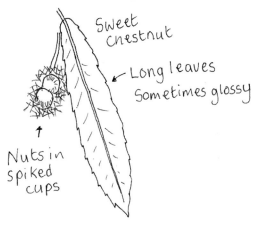

Sweet Chestnut

Long leaves Sometimes glossy

Nuts in spiked cups

When you collect them, cut a slit in the skin of all the nuts and leave them in a dry place – possibly a drawer. If you wish, a single, un-split chestnut can be kept so that, when it explodes, the rest of the batch will be ready to eat. The only problem with this is that they don't always explode and when they do they can make a bit of a mess. Keep them away from plastic bags too, as they will sweat and you will need to check them for insects and grubs too. They can be cooked and then frozen.

Health
Bach Flower Remedies sell sweet chestnut tincture for people who are 'at their limit of endurance and in deep despair' but they do not say why or how this works. Sweet chestnuts contain a very mild tranquilizer, similar to valerian and lettuce but, unlike most nuts, the chestnut is packed with carbohydrates, not fat. They are cholesterol-free, and low in sodium, making them a healthy option.

Peeling the skin
Cut a cross into the skin with a sharp knife, but watch your fingers. If it turns red you have cut your thumb!

Then boil them for three minutes and drain and cool. The skins should peel away quite easily.

Potato alternatives

You can boil chestnuts out of their skin until they are soft enough to puree. Mixed with a little milk and seasoning, they make a great alternative to mashed potato.

Roasting chestnuts is easy. Pop them on a metal plate by the fire if you have one. Alternatively, put them in a moderate oven at 175°C for 30 minutes. If they are still hard, just return them to the oven for another 15 minutes and recheck later. You can do this either in their shells or peel them first.

Chestnuts can be ground into a flour, which gives the tree one of its other names – the bread tree. The starch in the nut produces a wonderful bread, especially when mixed with rye and other seeds.

Chestnut bread

The Romans had huge fire houses packed to the rafters with chestnuts, which they lit a fire beneath. The chestnuts were then roasted for days and ground. The resulting flour was used to make both bread and cakes.

You can do the same by first boiling the chestnuts to help remove the skins. Then roast them for a couple of hours in a warm oven at 150°C. From there you can either puree the chestnuts and allow them to dry, or simply allow them to cook and feed them into a grinder.

Mix 50:50 with ordinary flour and use in your ordinary

bread recipe or make dough with the flour with a little water and a tablespoon of oil. Roll into tortillas and cook on a griddle or in a frying pan.

Marrons glace

You need a kilo of shelled and peeled chestnuts and the same quantity of sugar. Boil 500ml of water and carefully add the sugar, stirring until it is all dissolved. Put the chestnuts into the syrup and boil for ten minutes. Then remove them and leave to cool for 24 hours. Keep the syrup. Reheat the syrup the following day and, when boiling, add the chestnuts and boil for a further ten minutes. Repeat this process for three or four cycles.

After the chestnuts have cooled for the last time, place them on baking parchment and bake for two hours at 150°C.

Wild Cherry
Prunus avium

You will be surprised by this tree as it either bursts from hedges or in the centre of the deepest wood. It fills itself with flowers in the spring, either white or pink, depending on the nutrients available to it. It grows to about 15 metres, has oval serrated leaves and the fruits look just like the cherries you buy in the shops, but can be quite bitter.

The fruits are great for jams and preserves but need a lot of sugar. Cherry brandy is as likely as not their best use. Simply find a glass container that will take the brandy without leaking or evaporation. Then half fill it with stoned cherries. Top the whole container up with brandy and seal and forget.

Yew

Taxa ssp.

You (forgive the pun) are more likely to see Yew in a churchyard than anywhere else these days. This is because the Plantagenet kings (Remember them?) made it a law that every parish grew yews so that the nation would always have bows to fight the Scots and the French. They were planted in every churchyard because cattle ate the young saplings, and the churchyard was the only enclosed land in the area.

Yew is an interesting plant. It is not a gymnosperm, because it has an almost covered seed. It is not fully an angiosperm because the seed is not completely covered. The seeds themselves are poisonous, but Nature has provided us with a get out clause. The fleshy cup the covers nearly all the seed is not poisonous. Indeed, it is quite nice to eat. So to collect yew, pull the little dark seed from the centre of the fruit and then eat the red fleshy bit. It's lovely.

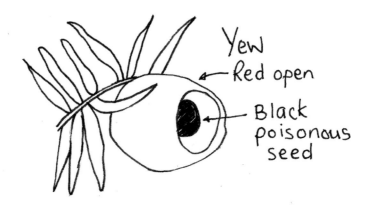

Yew
Red open
Black poisonous seed

2. On Heath and Hill

Now that we have reclaimed the right to roam over a countryside that has been closed for two hundred or more years, there is the opportunity to find all kinds of plants that are useful as food. Our culture of buying things to eat rather than growing our own or foraging has meant that we are now simply unaware of the great larder out there. But this has also led to some common misunderstandings too.

Buttercups, for example, are completely poisonous. They have been used as greens in times of severe hardship, but were boiled until all the poison had been completely destroyed. But what about buttercup syrup? Well, it is only a trade name; there is nothing but squill, a Mediterranean plant, capsicum and sugar in it. So don't think you can just take any old plant, just because you know its name.

Many of the plants you will meet on heath and hill are found elsewhere in this book, particularly the heather.

WARNING

Please be careful when you are foraging on fields, hillsides and meadows, especially in parkland. They are frequently sprayed by the local authorities to 'keep the weeds down' and the toxins can be accumulated in the plants that are no longer affected by our deathly chemical warfare. So please be sure that, when you do take plants to eat in the wild, especially on heath and hill, you are sure of the way the landscape has been used.

Chamomile
Chamaemelum nobile

Part of the extensive daisy family that is so useful. It bears lots of yellow, button sized daisy type flowers that are white and yellow. All the flowers look almost the same. The leaves are many lobed and acid green in colour. The plant is acidic and, if you chew the raw leaf, it might even cause blisters for some. However, it is a good remedy for colds, nuralgia and toothache. It is also good at relieving fevers, and the tea of the leaves is not only tasty (especially with a bit of honey in it), it is quite therapeutic too.

You will find chamomile growing almost anywhere, from the deepest valley to quite high on mountain tops and, since the television programme The Chamomile Lawn, it has become a common garden plant too.

As with many daisy plants the whole chamomile can be used to flavour beer.

Coltsfoot
Tussilago farfara

A dandelion lookalike, coltsfoot has odd shaped, roundish leaves that are green on one side and covered with hairs on the underside. Anyone older than me will remember coltsfoot rock. This is a candy sold by the chemist and eaten by children with bad chests. This is its main use, though the leaves can be boiled in stews and used as a vegetable. It does contain alkaloid chemicals that are poisonous to the liver, but these are broken down by cooking. To be on the safe side they should not be taken by pregnant or breastfeeding mums and young children.

The leaf should be removed from the boiling water and then rinsed in a colander with boiling water from the kettle. This makes them both safe and tasty. In hard times the leaves were dried and pounded to a powder to use as a salt substitute.

Daisy
Bellis perennis

Everyone knows the daisy, but just in case... It has large, white, compound flowers that close in the dark and open in the day. They can even sometimes have a purple element to them. The leaves look like an unmade bed, none of them being the same shape or colour. They are thickish and a little hairy with slightly serrated edges, that is to say there are not that many serrations, but the serrations are quite deep.

The leaves, either cooked or raw, are the edible part. You can simply pick them in the field and add them to your sandwich! You can cook them as a pot herb,in which case they fall about like spinach, or add a few to a salad.

Rough Hawkbit
Leontodon hispidus

You might be forgiven for mistaking this plant for a dandelion. It is slightly more slender and the flowers are not so full. But apart from this the leaves look almost exactly the same and they taste much the same too.

The leaves are not quite as good as dandelion for a salad, but they are good if you are able to mix them with other types of leaves and there is plenty of lemon juice. The roots, however, are used just in the same way as chicory by drying them out and powdering them as a coffee substitute. For this they are much better than dandelions, although none of these decoctions really tastes anything like coffee.

Salad Burnet
Sanguisorba minor

What an unusual plant! It is used these days to stop land workings that are long abandoned from eroding because the root system is so extensive and binds the soil. From a distance the leaves are like nettle leaves but with lots of edge serrations and they are borne doubly on either side of the stem.

They prefer chalky soil and, where forced to grow away from chalk, taste increasingly bitter. But still they are a fantastic addition to salads and can be boiled as a vegetable. In the summer, when they flower, the leaves become less tasty, so it is best to take it in the winter. The stems of the plant are angular and hairy, and dark red in colour towards the end.

Self Heal
Prunella vulgaris

This plant looks a little like lavender, the purple flowers on the end of the stalks resembling lavender flowers. The leaves are like spades on long handles, rounded at the back, pointed at the end and slender. They are green/yellow in colour.

It has a long history of medicinal use and is particularly good at reducing fevers, stopping bleeding and is really fantastic for sore throats and mouth infections. Simply place a few leaves in boiling water with a spoon of honey. It is fantastically soothing.

The leaves can be used in salads and stews, but are a little on the bitter side.

White Clover
Trifolium repens

Again, everyone is familiar with clover. The name Trifolium simply means three leaves, and that's just what this plant has. The whole plant can be used, but recent studies have shown that it should be cooked to remove a rather complex chemical chain of events that might sometimes lead to poisoning. However, white clover has been used for generations.

The dried leaves have a vanilla flavour and are usually ground into a powder and sprinkled on cakes, or in custard. The leaves can be boiled up like spinach, but they need to be collected before the plant is in flower.

The flower heads can be dried make a good tea which is said to help people with rheumatism.

Yarrow
Achillea millefolium

You cannot mistake yarrow because of the leaves. They are divided into hundreds of tiny leaflets, *millefolium* meaning thousands of leaves. They are borne on a central stalk and the impression you get is of a green mist when viewed from a long way off. The flowers are white, purpleish or yellow and are arranged in a loose umbel, but this plant is not a member of the *umbelliferae* (the parsley and carrot family), but is a member of the *compositae* or daisy family.

The leaves are used as a vegetable or a salad. They are rather bitter but make an interesting addition to a salad because the tiny leaflets actually absorb dressings rather well. You can also use them to flavour ale instead of hops, to make beer.

The leaves are also made into a restoring tea, which is said to ease both colds and menstrual pain.

3. Along the Riverbank

There are few things more pleasant than a stroll along the river, not just because of the flowing water, the lovely scenery and the plants. Rivers are cooling and calming things, each having their own temperament and life. More than anything, frequent visits to the river bring peace.

The wildlife beside the river is very pleasing too, and there are few pleasures in the world to equal sitting by flowing water, rod in hand, watching the water pass by. It is a truly civilised experience.

If you are foraging in or near a river, make sure you do not partake in the pleasure alone. Take a friend who will be able to secure your safety. Also, never reach over water and do not wade into anything deeper than your feet.

Himalayan Balsam
Impatiens glandulifera

This plant is the scourge of the riverside, with lots of pink flowers and long stems that grow to the exclusion of almost everything else. But bees love it and you see them collecting pollen like crazy, covered in the stuff as though they had been dipped in sherbet!

The plant is a relative of the busy Lizzie and the leaves contain oxalates that are destroyed on cooking, but the young leaves are lovely boiled and served with a knob of butter. I should only eat it once in the summer, but it is lovely.

Take the youngest leaves and ignore the fruits - if you can. When ripe the fruits 'explode,' throwing their seeds everywhere. In the fruit coat there are two tissues that, as they dry, get tighter and tighter, so that when they are fully taught the slightest touch makes them snap. Fantastic for frightening children! But then the seeds are added to the soil and the problem of this weed worsens.

Lady's Bedstraw
Galium verum

What a plant! This little beauty has angular, hairy stems that stick to your clothing. The leaves are borne in a circle all around the stem at the same point and are also 'sticky' and it bears yellow flowers at the top of the plant that make it look like a brightly stained, partially eaten candyfloss. The flowers themselves are almost cruciform (like a cross) and the anthers protrude in the spaces of the petals, of which there are four.

The whole plant can be chopped up, put into a muslin and used to curdle milk. It is one of the constituents of vegetarian rennet. The leaves are edible raw in salads or cooked as a vegetable. They also give a yellow dye. The seeds can be collected, roasted and ground to create a coffee substitute (actually, it's quite nice) and the flowers can be boiled in water, strained and then served cool with a spoon of honey for a great summer time drink.

Reedmace
Typha latiflora

I often think of Moses among the bulrushes, although he probably never saw one during the whole of his life. The common reedmace, or bulrush, is a very common and very edible plant. It does exist almost everywhere except for Africa and the Middle Eastern part of Southern Asia.

It forms great hedges of plants in slower moving waters and is consequently a great source of cover for all kinds of animals and, incidentally, is a brilliant hiding place for the pike and his cousin the zander.

Everyone knows what they look like. A reed that is at least a metre in height with very long leaves on either side. On the top is a brown, furry 'handle' that is really a collection of flowers, or inflorescence as botanists call it. They grow in profusion at the water's edge and will spread very quickly when the conditions are right.

It divides vegetatively at the root with seedswhich are also highly viable and, within a very short time, it takes over the whole bank, even stopping the water flow if allowed.

This whole plant is extremely useful and has been cultivated for centuries. The pollen, which is a protein rich additive to flour, has been used in fireworks because it is highly flammable. The flowers and seeds are edible, but have been used as pillow stuffers, nappy liners, life jackets and fire kindling too. The seeds are also very rich in oil.

As late as 100 years ago the stems were used as rush-lights. For this the outer leaves were trimmed, the root removed and the stem allowed to dry. They were then soaked in whatever fat or oil was available. When suspended from a wall mounting the rushlight, around 40cm long, gave a good light that was said to be better than a candle. It was certainly cheaper, if a little sootier and possibly a might more dangerous because the flame was invariably bigger too.

The thickened base of the stem, where the root is attached, was used as a vegetable, as were the young shoots. Known as Cossack Asparagus, the shoots were cleaned off and boiled. They are very nutritious and tasty. The root is also boiled like a potato and can be used as it is or mashed and has a light sweetness. It is very starchy but has a lot more protein than a potato, and is consequently much better for you.

In times of hardship the roots have been dried and pounded into a flour for making bread. Metre for metre, reedmace yields two to three times what our cereal crops provide, making this probably one of the best plants for mankind.

When you consider that the stems and leaves can also be soaked and beaten to produce paper and the stems make a great thatching material, and that you can make plastics from the macerated stems, this has to be the most versatile plants there is!

Sweet flag
Acorus calamus

This plant is naturalised in the UK and is nothing to do with the pretty flags, or irises, which are quite poisonous. The sweet flag is a bit like a grass with a rude looking flower spike that juts out of the side of a stem through the leaves.

There have been suggestions that this plant contains chemicals implicated in cancer but people have been using it for centuries with no visible side effects. The reason for including it here is that the leaves can be boiled to create a vegetable, and the rhizome, boiled in sugar, can be made into a candy. It is probably the best natural treatment for toothache there is.

Vervain
Verbena officinalis

Verbena means sacred plant, and it is a glory when you come across it. It grows in full sun by the river bank – particularly away from the actual water's edge. The flower head is a spike of little florets that appear from the bottom, and there are several of them on each plant. Individually the flowers are very pretty and there are five petals. Often mauve or lightly purple in colour, they give the impression of cornflowers in colour. The leaves are 10–15cm long and are like pointed fingers, or lanceolate, and the edges are very highly serrated or toothed.

It is the leaves that are useful. The plant has a restorative effect and the leaves have been dried out and used as a herbal tea for many thousands of years. The leaves are also made into a vegetable by simply boiling and adding a knob of butter and a little salt and pepper to them.

Watercress
Nasturtium officinale

This is the hallmark of a good clean river. In fast flowing water the mustard oil plant is a key species to find to convince you that the water is good, because pollution kills it off rather quickly. Interestingly, the large cress farms in the south of England are having the same effect because every time the plant is bruised or bashed about, it protects itself by releasing a sulphourous chemical to the water. This in turn kills some insects, particularly the food insects of trout, which in turn disappear downstream to the consternation of fishermen.

Watercress is a mass of stems and leaves. The leaves are kidney shaped around the stem and they bear tiny cruciferous flowers (four petals in the shape of a cross). They really only grow in flowing water where there is a lime element to the rock strata.

The plant is excellent at attracting wildlife, especially insects, and so, if you collect it in the wild, you need to put it into a bucket of fresh water and shake it about to dislodge anything. Do remember to pour the water back into the river.

The whole plant is useful and is far too nice to be used only as a garnish to be thrown aside at the end of the meal.

Watercress soup

1 large potato
1kg watercress
1 large onion
1 carrot
1 litre vegetable stock
50ml cream

Peel the vegetables and dice into small cubes. Remove the largest stalks from the watercress.

Sweat the chopped onion in a little oil and add the vegetables (but not the cress) and cook for 5 minutes. Add the stock and cook until the vegetables are tender. Add the cress and cook for a further 5 minutes. Blend with a hand blender and stir in the cream. Season to taste.

Fishing

This book is not designed as a treatise on fishing. It's not big enough for that purpose. But there is something to be said for learning how to fish. For a start, it opens a whole new aspect to your country walk. You begin to think about fish and predators and bottom feeders and currents and weeds. There are currently five million fishermen in the country, but they do not all take and eat their fish. Personally I cannot think of any reason for pulling a fish out of the water, unless you are intending to eat it.

When a fish takes a hook we are led to believe that it invariably goes into its lip and that this lip is so horny the fish never feels a thing. Not so, the fish usually sucks the hook into its mouth and then quite naturally swallows. A good number of hooks go right down into the gut or become caught in soft tissue. The only reason for inflicting such an indignity can be for food, well for me at least.

I have no problem with fishing in order to get better at it, and to learn about fishing and the fish you catch in order that, at a later date, you can get really good at catching fish for food.

The only other motivation I can offer you is twofold. Firstly, freshwater fish is not muddy, devoid of taste and boring. Some of the best meals you can get are freshwater fish. Secondly, the fish you buy in the supermarket are often bad for the environment and bad for the fish. Imagine having the sea bed vacuumed by a trawler, completely messing up a ten metre wide stretch by several miles long. Then imagine a fish in such a net being pulled out of the water and slowly crushed to death with the rest allowed to suffocate in air for many minutes.

There is every reason to believe that people who fish for their own food are doing fishkind a good turn.

Eel

For ages and ages, eels have been the mainstay of the poor, and this is because the poor had a very good method of catching eels without the rich finding out which, if they had, would have meant trouble. This method also ensured the biggest and fattest eels would be caught, and probably more than one at that.

First of all you need a large sack. A postal sack is a

good size, but the bigger, the better. You also need a way of keeping the neck of the sack open. A hoola-hoop will usually suffice. In the bottom of the sack is placed a brick which will allow it to sink. Then the carcass of a chicken after you have finished with it, leaving just a little for the fish to nibble. The rest of the sack should be packed with loose straw up to just over half way. At the mouth end of the trap you attach a really good rope that is at least 15 metres long and, to the end of this, make an anchor so it can be fastened to the riverbank.

This is thrown into the river and secured to the bank. After 24 hours it can be checked. It might take a couple of days to catch, but when it does you can guarantee a good catch. The best water to put it in is the deeper water with a slow moving current.

Killing an eel is more difficult than you might think. You have to give it a good bash on the back of the head with a 'priest.' There are plenty of tales of eels swimming around in the frying pan! Another way of killing eels is to put them in a container of water along with a couple of handfuls of salt. This will also remove the slime from the skin, with which eels are completely covered.

You need to wash the fish for 30 minutes in many changes of water and then gut it. This is done by cutting from just before the vent on the underside, all the way up to the head. This way you will get the kidneys and the gut out in one go. Trim the skin away if you prefer and then cut into fillets across the backbone. You cannot properly fillet an eel like an ordinary fish.

Jellied eels

This was a popular dish that was highly favoured in Southern England. Originally it only applied to eels which, when boiled with their bones intact, produced a jelly. The jelly would preserve the fish for about a week, particularly if salted. Nutmeg is used in most recipes. Cut the eel into four-inch strips, roll it with the skin outermost and tie with string before you boil them in a liquor made from fish stock or water with a little chopped onion and celery.

4. Beach and Sea

It is possible to live forever on a beach if the sea is in decent condition. Some places are just a dead loss for anything because the sea is so polluted, although this is beginning to get better as time goes by and the water companies spend more of the money they get on decent sewage treatment works. Also there are nuclear facilities of one sort and another dotted around the coast and, despite their best efforts to reassure us they are safe, I simply cannot bring myself to forage near them. Perhaps this is as well because the wild places are best left alone, even if there are a few million tonnes of concrete and uranium nearby.

When I was a student on a marine biology component of my course, my friends and I decided to live only on what could be found on the beach. We collected material on the island of Anglesey, sometimes near large(ish) villages and towns and probably ate rather too much human effluent in the process. We certainly spent a lot of time in the smallest room. But when we collected from the remote beaches, we had a wonderful time eating some of the best food I believe you can get anywhere!

There are two morals to the tale, both to be repeated time and again so you won't forget them. Firstly, don't collect seafood near human occupancy unless you have a cast iron gut or shares in a toilet roll company. Secondly, never eat anything that has died itself. Whatever killed it is also likely to do the same to you!

One last thing; remember you are human. We are (hopefully) compassionate and civilised creatures. One of the most upsetting things for me is people being all macho and eating live animals as if they have to prove themselves. Cook everything you eat. The rapid killing of the animal is a blessing for it (compared to being chewed up in the mouth or slowly digested in the stomach) and it's much healthier for you too.

The beach really starts at the high water mark, but this doesn't mean to say we cannot walk a little beyond it to get a nibble.

Plant Life

Beta vulgaris

This plant forms clumps in shingle and sand and looks just like ordinary garden beet – which in a way it really is. The leaves are glossy, the stalks red and the flowers appear like little green buds on thick long stalks, a bit like millet, for those who keep budgies.

The leaves can be collected and used like any greens.

They are sometimes eaten raw but make an excellent spinach type meal. The plant becomes more bitter as the leaves get older, but this bitterness is removed on cooking.

Dulse

Dulse looks a little like porphyra but is distinctly red in colour. Many of our red algae are endangered species, so please don't collect them willy-nilly. Dulse, however, is quite common. It is to be found mostly in rock pools clinging to rocks in the water. You will do best to collect only the perfect ones, and be aware that a basket full boils down to just a couple of servings. Dulse often has a long frond and a lot of 'baby' ones growing all around the sides of it.

Simply plunge it in boiling water then freeze it. You can dry it and re-hydrate it as you need it.

Dulse soda bread

450g self raising flour
Level teaspoon salt
Level teaspoon baking powder
284ml carton buttermilk
A good handful of dulse

Preheat oven to 220°C, Gas mark 7. Grease a baking tray with a little oil. Sift flour, salt and baking powder together in a large mixing bowl. Cut the dulse into strips and incorporate into the flour. Stir in buttermilk and bind to a soft dough. The mixture should be a little sticky. Add a little more milk or water if the mixture seems dry.

Form into a round and place on a baking tray, cutting across the top of the loaf to make four sections. Bake for 20-25 mins till golden brown.

Porphyra

These days porphyra is grown commercially in Japan. Probably, should you have a Welsh breakfast in a B&B, which incidentally is just like an English one but with some fried porphyra on the plate, the seaweed element has come from the Far East. But most rocky beaches have enough of the plant for a good few meals.

This is a brown seaweed known as Bara Lawr, or lava bread. It looks like a thin, almost translucent, olive brown tissue that, when the sea is out, falls and covers the rock to which it is secured. It is most likely to be found half way down the beach amongst a lot of other algae.

When you collect the plant, keep it cool and wet – preferably in a wicker basket that you can splash from time to time. As with dulse you will need a big basket full to get a couple of meals out of it.

Firstly, take it home and boil it as quickly as you can. It doesn't need cooking for long, just a couple of minutes, and if you can carry seawater home, all the better. Drain the seaweed and then squeeze it as dry as possible. Place it in the freezer until you need it.

The seaweed can be used in soups, but almost invariably it is pressed into cubes and fried in the pan after bacon has been cooked in it. It takes on the flavour of the bacon and is quite delicious!

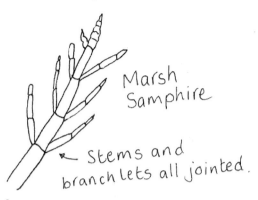

Marsh
Samphire

Stems and
branchlets all jointed.

Marsh Samphire
Salicornia europea

There is a very common confusion between rock samphire and marsh samphire – a totally different species. I don't suppose it really matters that much, but it is good to get things right. This one looks like a miniature cactus which is probably the best way to describe it.

The rock samphire grows near the sea on rocks and was once a very common vegetable. It was shipped to the cities in barrels each spring and the craze would continue until it had all been eaten up. Because of its saltiness, it was usually served with fish. The plant is actually quite rare and has been collected heavily over the years, so please do not collect too much. If you find a large strand, a handful is all you need. You can now grow your own samphire too, and it is quite unusual because you will have to add salt to it.

Blanch for a minute in unsalted water (it's salty enough when from the sea). A dressing of 4:1 olive oil to lemon juice is drizzled over the warm vegetable and a few shavings of Parmesan cheese sprinkled over the top.

Rock Samphire
Crithmum maritimum

A completely different plant containing a lot of silica. It is edible, but to my mind not very nice to eat. It looks a little like marsh samphire but is more open, less jointed, and does not have the dichotomous dividing that the other samphire has.

This is simply collected, steamed for a few minutes and served with fish. It is also known as the asparagus of the sea.

Sea buckthorn
Hippophae rhamnoides

This plant is classed in the super food category for all sorts of reasons. Firstly, it is packed with vitamins C and A. Secondly, although tart, it is delicious.

It is to be found off the coast in sheltered parts of Southern England and extensively along the east coast. A huge bush, it grows to 6 metres in some places. The tiny fruits are 6-8mm in diameter and borne along the stems. They are usually crushed for their juice.

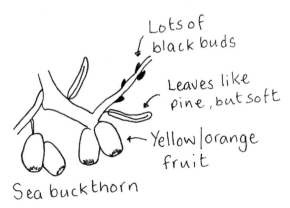

Lots of black buds

Leaves like pine, but soft

Yellow/orange fruit

Sea buckthorn

Sea holly

Steel/blue flowers and leaves.

Sea Holly
Eryngium maritimum

The sea holly looks like a cross between a thistle and a holly and it grows in sand beyond the high water mark. It is a blue coloured plant with spiney leaves and the flowers look like big thistles.

The young leaves are edible and, when boiled, are supposed to taste like asparagus. The roots, which grow to profusion and lie deep in the sand, are excellent when roasted. Treat them as though they were parsnips and roast them in the oven for 45 minutes at 180°C or until soft. The sugars will caramelise and it is very tasty.

Two hundred years ago the plants were collected en masse and turned into aphrodisiac lozenges by boiling the stems, leaves and roots in sugar. Since it is a good diuretic, the lozenges were an excellent treatment for gout, for which they were prized.

Sea Purslane
Halimione portulacoides

This plant looks like a low growing bush. The leaves are olive green and look like fat lolly sticks, often oval with many of them borne on the stems. The leaves are succulent and crunchy to bite and are best cooked with melted butter and seasoning.

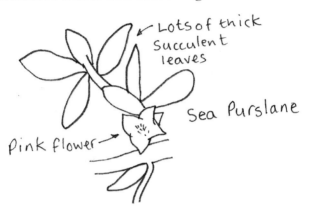

Sea Thrift
Armeria maritima

The tiny pink thrift flowers in strands on rocks in exposed places and make the seaside really pretty. The plant lies flat on the ground with the flowers borne like candy floss sticks about it. It grows on the very most exposed parts of the rocks, cliffs and hills around the beach and prefers a sandy soil, so it is very good at coping with drought conditions.

The plant has been used as an antibiotic for a long time, and has also been used to treat nervous disorders, but little actual medical study has been carried out. It has also been used for the treatment of obesity.

Sea thrift

Large (4cm) balls of flowers.

Grass-like leaves

Watch for seagulls who nest nearby.

The leaves and root can be cooked as a vegetable, but it would be a shame to collect all the thrift in a particular locality because it is very slow growing. Although this plant has been prescribed to help people with weight loss diets, it is probably the fact that you have to go on a long walk to find and collect it which is probably the best way of losing weight.

Zostra

Zostra marina

If you look at the low water mark and see something that looks like grass, this is zostra, or eel grass. It is collected the world over for food, except in the UK. In Scandinavia it represents the largest crop of the littoral zone and hundreds of thousands of tonnes are cropped annually. It is the only salt water grass that we know of, and where it occurs it can be found in great swathes. The plant grows up to 30cm tall and simply looks like grass. It needs a good wash before it is used.

The plant can be blended into soups and added to

salads, but is probably best cooked.

Seaweeds

Seaweeds come in three basic types: red, green and brown. Most of the browns are edible. The reds are less edible, and are also rare. The green algae are also edible, but more troublesome. On the whole the green seaweeds like to live where there is an outfall of fresh water mingling with the salt water. Part of the day they are covered by sea, part of the day they are covered, or at least splashed, by fresh water. The problem with this is the quality of the fresh water.

Often any fresh water falling onto a beach from the surrounding countryside is contaminated with waste from the inhabitants, especially so if the locality is rural. Before eating any green seaweed, make sure of the water that is falling on it.

The long, leathery seaweeds, sometimes upwards of 3 metres long, are called Laminaria. There are some basic types, one with a lot of fronds attached to a stem which is then in turn attached to a pebble. The fronds make a sail and the plant travels the oceans like some ghostly sailing ship. The other one, with a single frond, does exactly the same, only there is a single sail, and this is all wrinkled.

Along their length you will see discoloured parts of the frond, and sometimes the ends will be white. These are dead. The golden rule is that you never, ever eat anything from a beach that is already dead. You have to kill it yourself. This also goes for seaweed and plants as well as animals.

By the way, both of these, Laminaria digitalis (the one with the many fronds) and Laminaria saccahrina (the one with the single frond) are edible. The second, if you haven't already guessed, used to be a source of the well known sweetener.

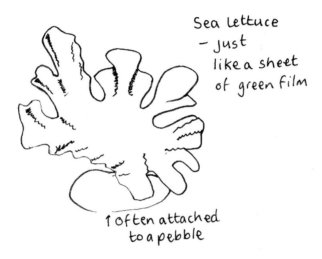

Sea Lettuce
– Just like a sheet of green film

↑ often attached to a pebble

The sea lettuce
Ulva lactuca

This is a green one and looks just like a very thin, very green lettuce leaf. You often get a thin sheet that is quite large, sometimes as big as your hand. It is called sea lettuce because it looks like a lettuce, not because it tastes like one. Nor is it any good in a salad. It is best used collected, washed and dried and then cut into strips and fried in hot oil for no longer than a minute. A close relative of the sea lettuce is a seaweed that looks like green tubes and is called Enteromorpha intestinalis. It is very common, especially where a stream falls onto the beach, so be sure of the quality of the water! This should simply be patted dry and deep fried for less than a minute.

Shellfish

Cockles

Cockles live in large areas of mud flats, on the sides of estuaries, and on open sandy areas of the inter-tidal zone. They feed in shallow water and bury themselves under the surface when the tide goes out, which makes them relatively easy to rake up. If you are going to do this, however, watch out for fast incoming tides and quicksand and get as much information as you can about the area.

Cockles are exported to the Far East by the hundreds of tonnes, yet we should be eating them ourselves. You will need a stout wooden rake and you should collect a bucket full in about an hour – enough for ages!

> Boil the cockles for a couple of minutes and then work out the flesh into a jar of vinegar. An hour's work will provide you with pizza toppings and the very best steak and kidney pie additives for a couple of months.

Cockle- usually forces its 'tongue' out.

Limpet

Slightly off-centre hump. Attached to rocks.

Limpets

You see these molluscs clinging to rocks. They look like little kneecaps, which is what their scientific name, Patella vulgaris, referrs to – the vulgar kneecap! They make good eating and resemble other seashore molluscs. To get at them you need a stout pair of boots, and you should collect them just as the tide has come away from them. Give them a tap and you should see them close themselves down on the rock. Choose only the ones you see moving. Then give them a swift kick with the heel of the boot. They will come away to reveal the animal beneath.

Boil them straight away if you can, in some salted water, and the flesh will come away from the inner shell. Only boil them for a minute, which is just enough time to kill them.

Limpets in garlic butter

This is served in tapas bars all over Spain. Over there they cut the mollusc out of the shell before killing it, but I prefer to kill it in boiling water first. Collect about 20 shells and plunge them into boiling water. Drain and remove them from their shells and put 75g butter and a tablespoon of olive oil in a frying pan. Add as many crushed garlic cloves as you like – say 4, and three finely chopped shallots.

When the shallots are just translucent, add the limpets and stir in well. Cook for a minute or so and add a handful of chopped parsley. To enhance this dish, a glass of white wine, reduced for a couple of minutes, makes a wonderful addition. Or even a tub of cream, or both! Season to taste.

Mussels

Mussels are found on jetties and piers and attached to rocks. All you have to do is pull them off, but first check the sewage status of the beach. They will keep fresh in a bit of ice – one of those insulated picnic boxes with a couple of frozen bars inside is sufficient. Do not take ones that are already open, these are dead. If you tap them you should be able to see them tighten up.

It is possible to cook and kill mussels at the same time because they die very easily under a slight heat.

Mussels in Wine

This dish can be adapted, replacing mussels with anything available. The sauce tastes like concentrated sea-side, and whereas we use wine in this recipe, you could go mad and use brandy.

A large, finely chopped onion
30g butter
Garlic, 2 to 3 cloves, finely crushed
15g flour
Half a bottle of white wine
300ml double cream
800g mussels
Chopped parsley

First melt the butter in a steep sided pan and sweat off the onions and garlic until they are translucent, after which you sprinkle the flour into the butter mix to thicken. Stir well to avoid lumps, and continue to cook for another three minutes.

Slowly add the wine, stirring all the time. Continue to stir until the sauce begins to thicken.

Add the mussels to the sauce and shake the pan well to settle the contents. Immediately cover with a lid and turn up the heat. The wine is now steaming the mussels, and this should take between 12 and 15 minutes to complete. Check the dish and stir every few minutes, replacing the lid each time.

When all the shells are open, turn down the heat and slowly add the cream, stirring and allowing the sauce to thicken. Finally, season and add a generous amount of parsley. Serve with freshly baked bread.

Razor clam

These are great little molluscs that look like cut-throat razors. Inside the long, double shells is a soft bodied mollusc that is quite edible and tastes of the sea shore. They live in sand, just above the low tide mark.

The razor clam, not to be confused with the lugworm, has small circular indentations the size of a £2 coin. If you place a teaspoon of salt on what looks like a tiny water filled hole, the clam will come shooting out and all you have to do is pop it in your bucket. About 10 will make for two decent portions.

Again, as for everything I collect on the beach, pop it in some boiling water for a minute to kill the animal. You can then open the shells and remove the white meat. It is wonderful fried up with bacon., and in particular with spiced sausages such as choritzo.

Razor clam with cheese and wine

This is a great one for a seafood pasta. For an accompaniment choose something like linguini.

Take ten clams and immerse them in boiling water for 1 minute. Open out and remove the white flesh, which you cut into 1cm pieces. Sweat a handful of finely diced shallots with 50g butter and a tablespoon of extra virgin olive oil in a pan and add a couple of crushed garlic cloves. Then add your pieces of clam. Almost straight away add a large glass of white wine and 250g strong cheddar cheese. Stir constantly until the cheese, wine and shallots are all melted together. Simply serve into your favourite pasta.

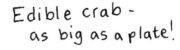

Edible crab -
as big as a plate!

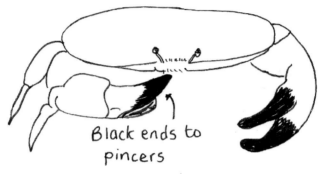

Black ends to
pincers

Crabs and shrimps

I imagine that almost everyone has loaded a crab line with pieces of bacon and pulled out a prickly little green beast. No more than a few inches across and holding on for dear life with one of its claws, it skittles immediately across the sand and back into the sea.

There are two crabs found on our shores worth collecting for food. All the rest are either too small or too full of toxins because they prefer to eat near waste pipes. The edible crab is usually as big as a small dinner plate and has a red, sandy body with black tips to the claws, and the spider crab looks pretty much like a large, alien spider.

Edible crabs are usually collected by putting a little bait in a netted box into which the crab can climb, but from which it cannot escape. The traps are quite cheap to buy and, if you have a boat to sink one to the bottom of around twenty feet of water, you will be able to catch a crab a day for your dinner.

You can hunt both edible and spider crabs at low tide by lifting stones near the shoreline. They will not resist being collected, and are quite safe to pick up from the back. Spider crabs congregate in large numbers at low tide in the winter in the southern counties of England, and are packed with good meat.

All crustaceans should, wherever possible, be narcotised before killing. This is done by placing them in the freezer for at least two hours. They can then be plunged into boiling water where they will feel no pain and death will be immediate.

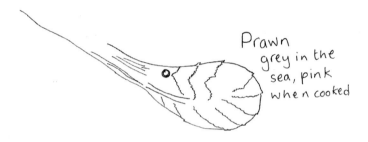

Prawn grey in the sea, pink when cooked

Shrimping can still be done on all our shores where pollution levels are within safe limits. The basic tool is a push net, so called because you push it along. It is wide, sturdy and in the shape of a 'D.' The net is pushed along the floor of the sea at a depth of a foot or so and, after a short while, enough shrimps for a mouthful can be collected easily. An afternoon's work should provide enough shrimps to make a curry. But you will also catch other marine creatures from shore crabs to small fish.

Potted shrimp

Easy! Boil your shrimps and drain. Push them into a

ramekin and force as many as you can into the pot. Melt some butter and add a big pinch of salt and some pepper, filling the pot with the hot seasoned butter. Finish with a pinch of cayenne.

If you go a little further out and sweep the beach with the water at waist height you are likely to collect Dover sole and sand eel too. The eel can be thrown back, but the Dover sole should be killed and eaten – poached with a slice of lemon.

There are few better seashore picnics than freshly boiled shrimps. Use a large pan of boiling seawater and toss the shrimps in so that they are killed outright. Then peel and eat! Fantastic.

Sea fish

Don't worry, you are not being asked to become a fisherman, but with a little help and the guts to go and talk to other fishermen you find on the seashore, you can stock yourself up with all sorts of great food.

Mackerel

When the water is warming up you can start catching mackerel. You catch them on feathers – which are shiny looking lures that you buy from the bait shop. They can have up to six hooks on them. You simply cast them out and then slowly pull them in. On most casts you will catch fish. You can spend the whole day (or night) casting in the fresh air from any rock at the beach of your choice!

When you have caught your fish you will need to kill it. Keep a priest to hand but not for last rites!. This is basically a club which delivers the last rites, although this isn't why it's called a priest. As soon as you get the fish out of water, preferably BEFORE you take the fish off the hook, hit it sharply on the head twice with the priest. This will kill the fish and end its agony.

Cut the dorsal fin from the fish's back with a pair of scissors. Then remove the heads behind the gills and also the tail. You will need a very sharp, stout knife for this.

On the belly of the fish, insert the knife into what would have been the fish's bottom with the blade facing outwards. Draw the knife all the way up the belly, dividing the fish into two. Repeat the manoeuvre, opening up the tail end.

Because the head and tail have already been removed the gut will fall out of the fish, especially if encouraged to do so with the thumb. Wash the inside under the cold tap.

To fillet the fish, cut along its back until you feel the backbone. Continue to draw the knife to one side of the backbone, paring away the flesh and leaving the bones behind. You will get the odd bone left in the fillet, but these can easily be removed with a pair of tweezers. Repeat the process for the other half of the fish.

Once you have your fillets there are many recipes for them. You can roll them up, pierce them with a cocktail stick and soak them in spiced, peppered vinegar, when they are called rollmops. You could coat them in seasoned oatmeal and fry them lightly in butter. Or you could finely grate garlic over fillets that have been

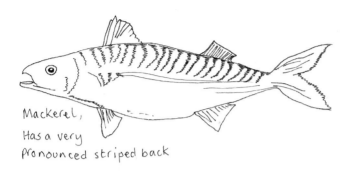

Mackerel,
Has a very
Pronounced striped back

brushed with a little olive oil and grill them for three minutes. The list is simply endless.

Mackerel Frito Misto

This is nothing more than a plate of fried fish, and should have herring fillets as a major constituent. Include also sardines, whitebait and a good quality cod or haddock cut into generously sized cubes. Simply fry the fish individually and drain onto a kitchen towel. The whitebait can be fried by the handful. Place them in a plastic bag with a good tablespoon of seasoned flower. Close the neck of the bag and lightly shake to incorporate the flower and fish. Empty the whitebait into your frying basket and carefully plunge into extremely hot oil until golden brown.

Serve all the fish together with a green salad and tartar sauce. Lovely!

Grilled mackerel and Garlic Salad

Grill the fillets and, when cool, flake the meat into a dish, adding grated garlic and a dash of olive oil. Mash with a fork and season with pepper.

Chapter Six
Wild Game - A Real Treat

Food from the wild does not always involve the picking of a few leaves and making nice salads. We have already looked at some fish, though we did say this book would not be a treatise on fishing. Similarly there are mammals and birds galore to be had, though legislation designed to keep the best for the person who owns the land means that you will need permission to take any food from it.

We do not have the space to deal with foods such as deer and large game such as geese but rabbit is a different matter. Now there's tasty! And we can go into the field and 'bag' a large number of rabbits for the pot. Of course it means you have to go out with the intention of getting food, so this is not just a walk in the woods. You will still need the landowner's permission, but if he is a farmer it is usually given all too readily because rabbits are fast becoming a sustainable population again after the ravages of myxomatosis.

Rabbits are scrupulously clean. They live exclusively on green plants and will not forage among litter or pollution. Of course they are cute and people do keep them as pets, hence our squeamishness about eating what has been for many centuries the salvation of the nation's poor. Quite why rabbit stew is not our national dish instead of bacon and eggs or a Sunday roast is a mystery to me. Perhaps it is because it is associated with poverty, and consequently people do not wish to be seen eating it? This foolishness will soon pass when economics dictate.

Do be careful and learn how to do this at the hands of an expert. Whether you use an air rifle, a bullet or a ferret with a mist net, the animal you are going to kill for your dinner is no sport. It might be fun, as all food collection should be, but it should be careful, compassionate fun, both for the treatment of the rabbit and the safety of the people around you.

There are really only two ways of killing a rabbit. One of those methods is with a free bullet (preferably a .22 from a rifle) although the most powerful airguns will do a good job as long as you have a head shot. Shooting the animal is within the law and is specified as being 'in the field' which exempts it from having to be stunned because the bullet stuns and kills at the same time.

This doesn't literally have to be in a field, but should be in a position where the bullet will exit only into soil, without injuring any other animal or person. The animal's neck should be sliced through to cut the jugular vein as soon as possible, within no more than than a few seconds, to allow it to bleed.

Animals caught by the common use of mist netting or using ferrets, can still be killed by neck dislocation. It is important that any dogs accompanying you are trained only to drive the rabbits into nets and not to attack them. This would be illegal under the 'hunting with dogs legislation.'

The back legs are held in one hand and the head cupped in the other, in a backwards position so that the fingers are near the ears. Holding tightly, the animal is stretched by pulling with both hands until the neck breaks. This is exactly the same as for a chicken. The knee can be used if the length of the rabbit makes it difficult to easily extend the arm. The rabbit should then be bled immediately by severing the neck.

The carcass is cleaned of its organs (including the head) and quartered, just like the old fashioned death penalty. The skin is removed, the legs chopped off and the hips and shoulders separated. The meat can be removed from the bone, or alternatively roasted as is. Rabbit roast is probably my own personal favourite.

Rabbit roast

You need half a quartered rabbit per person. Drizzle the pieces with oil and place in a large roasting tray along with dozens (yes, dozens!) of garlic cloves still in their skins, chopped carrots, small raw potatoes, chopped parsnips, turnips and any other vegetables you have to hand. Salt everything liberally and drizzle the veg with oil and then put into a slow oven at 175°C until the rabbit is cooked, which should be just when the potatoes are soft.

Roadkill

There is a growing movement of people who eat animals hit by cars. Everything from tiny mammals to deer is regularly taken home for the pot. As usual there are some safeguards you need to bear in mind.

Firstly, it is illegal to take animals you have killed yourself. This is clearly an attempt at stopping people from driving like killing machines at any passing wildlife.

Secondly, just because you have killed it, or found it dead, it isn't necessarily yours. In law it still has an owner and, in the case of a deer or a sheep, it has a value too! You should, by law, try to find the owner of the animal before removing it to the freezer.

Thirdly, just because it's still warm, it doesn't mean it is good to eat. You should use great caution before scraping something off the floor and cooking it up. Besides, how do you know that the animal was killed by a car. Perhaps it was impaired by some other problem, possibly a disease that would render it unfit for human consumption?

Finally, your car is not the place to put a dead, fat sheep which is most likely gushing both blood and other liquids, and the roadside is certainly not the place to gut and skin an animal. You need to be prepared for the eventualities before they appear, not afterwards.

The Good Life Press
P O Box 536
Preston
PR2 9ZY
01772 652693

The Good Life Press publishes a wide range of titles for the smallholder, farmer and country dweller as well as Home Farmer, the monthly magazine aimed at anyone who wants to grab a slice of the good life - whether they live in the country or the city.

Other titles of interest

A Guide to Traditional Pig Keeping by Carol Harris
An Introduction to Keeping Cattle by Peter King
An Introduction to Keeping Sheep by J. Upton/D. Soden
Build It! by Joe Jacobs
Cider Making by Andrew Lea
First Find a Field by Rosamund Young
Flowerpot Farming by Jayne Neville
Grow and Cook by Brian Tucker
How to Butcher Livestock and Game by Paul Peacock
Making Jams and Preserves by Diana Sutton
Precycle! by Paul Peacock
Showing Sheep by Sue Kendrick
Talking Sheepdogs by Derek Scrimgeour
The Bread and Butter Book by Diana Sutton
The Cheese Making Book By Paul Peacock
The Polytunnel Companion by Jayne Neville
The Sausage Book by Paul Peacock
The Shepherd's Companion by Jane Upton
The Smoking and Curing Book by Paul Peacock
The Urban Farmer's Handbook by Paul Peacock

www.goodlifepress.co.uk
www.homefarmer.co.uk